THE POWER OF NOW

POWER OF NOW: A COMPLETE PRACTICAL
GUIDE TO SELF-FREEDOM AND SELF-DISCIPLINE

By

AMBRACOM

Table of Contents
✶ ✶ ✶ ✶ ✶

Introduction. 1

Chapter 1: Your Mind and You. 5

  Freedom and Thought 7

    The Thinker and the Observer 7

    True Nature 9

  Understanding the Observer 11

    New Consciousness 11

    Thought 12

    Body and Mind. 13

  A Practical Exercise. 14

Chapter 2: Eliminating Stress and Empowering Yourself 17

  Pain 18

    The Ego and Fear 18

    Shining a Light 19

  Imagination 21

    Setting the Thinker Straight 21

    The Self. 23

  The Key to Defeat Anxiety. 24

    The Self Image. 25

Chapter 3: Understanding Your Existence. 29

  Zen and You. 30

    The Spirit of Zen. 30

    Transiency 32

    Mindfulness and Emptiness 33

Attachment 35

Practice 36

Chapter 4: The Tyranny of Time 41

The Nature of Time. 42

Time and Now 43

Communication from Nature. 44

Accessing True Power. 45

Letting Go of Pain 46

You Are Not Your Current Condition. 47

Achieving Goals 48

Chapter 5: Mental Traps to Beware of 51

Mind Tricks 52

Acceptance…and Nothing Else 52

The Present as a Means to the Future 53

Waiting. 55

Need to Understand the Past 56

Purpose 57

An Exercise. 59

Chapter 6: Understanding You. 61

Your Body and You 62

The Inner You 63

Transformation. 64

Your Body and the Now 66

The Aging Process 67

The Importance of Surrender 68

Chapter 7: Understanding Presence 71

Enhancing the Presence 72

Deep Roots 72

The Creative Mechanism. 73

Perception and Thought 74

Creative Flashes 75

Physical Elements of Presence. 77

Posture. 77

Breath. 78

Your Need to Control. 78

Practice 80

Chapter 8: Understanding Relationships. 83

Love and Romance 84

Love to Love/Hate 85

Addiction. 86

Healthy Relationships 87

Practice. 89

You and Your Partner. 90

You and the Collective. 91

You 92

Chapter 9: Understanding Peace 95

Drama. 96

The Way to Peace 96

Impermanence 97

Compassion 100

Reality 100

Conclusion 103

Introduction

Anytime one begins to write a book like this, the inevitable question pops up: What is the 'self'? What is the nature of 'I'? The reasons for you deciding to read this book are many. People across the globe have all kinds of problems in their daily lives, and at some point, everyone begins to ask the eternal question: What is my role in all of this?

It can be a scary question to ask. If you happen to be at a crossroads in your life, then the answer to this question taken on a grand significance. It will seem as if every decision you make from here on out will either lead to chaos or prosperity. Looking at the world in binary, that is as a have or have not, positive or negative, black or white, form is one of the hallmarks of a mind that isn't trained or wise enough to contemplate its own magnificence.

This is not meant to hurt you in any way. It's just that whatever your goal is, whether it be peace or self-discipline or achieving the elusive sense of freedom, you must begin by acknowledging the nature of your mind and where, in terms of evolution, it stands. Western society is a wonderful thing in so many ways. The freedoms and facilities that we enjoy are the envy of much of the world.

However, in so many ways, Western society is many light years behind ancient Eastern societies, it's a wonder we've made progress at all! Take, for instance, the widespread belief that human beings are at the pinnacle of evolution. There are several issues with this line of thought. First, being humans ourselves, how can we pass judgment on what the pinnacle of evolution is?

1

One recalls the wonderful quote from The Hitchhiker's Guide to the Galaxy by Douglas Adams, that says that man believes himself the most intelligent thanks to developing the wheel, New York and so on, while all the dolphins did was splash around in the water. In contrast, dolphins believe they're the most intelligent for precisely the same reasons.

Substitute the word intelligence for evolution, and you have the same scenario. Acceptance of ambiguity and the lack of a definite answer is a major weakness in Western societies. We're simply not equipped to deal with uncertainty and situations where outcomes are not clear. This is especially true when it comes to us. The current Millennial generation is discovering this first-hand.

The socioeconomic conditions into which a Millennial has entered is very different from what America and the west have traditionally offered. Jobs are present, but given the scary levels of debt, one needs to assume to land one, the pay is almost moot. The net result is a generational war of sorts between conservative older folk, who believe the kids are lazy, and the younger folk who believe the older people screwed things up.

This book is not going to solve global economic problems, far from it. However, given the anxiety and stress-ridden world of today, it pays to step back and examine our place in everything. Man's first instinct in the search for meaning is to look outward. The truth is if you wish to discover the secrets of life, nature, and the universe, all you need to do is look inward.

Man is as much a part of nature as a tree or a mountain. We're all part of the same ecosystem of life that has been created. We have forgotten this fact for a long time and have gotten carried away by our ability to seemingly master nature and 'conquer' it. This is akin to walking into a restaurant, moving a few chairs around and proclaiming yourself master of the premises. Few people would engage in such behavior.

INTRODUCTION

Yet, this is precisely how we behave, as a society, when it comes to nature. The underlying reason for all this a disconnect and it puts us at odds with nature. You see, we ourselves are a representation of nature. By opposing nature or seeking to conquer it, we're only harming ourselves.

This book will teach you how to reconnect and discover yourself. Discovering the order of things and their attendant meaning is nothing more than discovering yourself. Nature is represented in you. Understand your true nature, and you'll understand nature.

As a clarification, this book's aim is not to help you discover your life's purpose or teach you how to attract prosperity. Those aims will take care of themselves only when you understand higher principles. The highest principle for you to understand is the nature of your mind and "I". Your issues with discipline and stress and anxiety, all emanate from a lack of understanding of these things.

We will begin by understanding what your mind really is and your relationship with it. This leads us nicely into exploring the reasons for stress and empowering yourself by taking back control of your mind, in a practical, easy to understand manner. The rest of the book is concerned with teaching you the importance of presence.

This does not refer to charisma or any such thing, but merely the act of being aware of and living in the present moment. The 'now.' This affects everything from your relationships, to the nature of peace and awareness. We will also look at some tips and tricks to help you stay focused on the present moment, which is the ultimate act of self-discipline.

So, without further ado, let us begin our journey of discovery.

CHAPTER 1

Your Mind and You

Have you heard the story about how circuses back in the day used to train their elephants to not run amok and stay chained to their spots? Well, this is what they used to do. When the elephant was still a baby, they would tie its legs with an extremely strong chain to a post.

As hard as it would try to thrash and pull against the chain, the little elephant would not be able to get the pole to budge or the chain to break. Eventually, after many years of struggle, a day would come when the elephant would simply stop trying and resign itself to the fact that the thing around its ankles was unbreakable.

At this point, the trainers would remove the chain from the elephant's leg and unshackle it from the pole. They would then tie a piece of string around its leg and loosely tie the other end to a stake in the ground. Would the elephants ever break free? No, they never would, unless they happened to lose their minds.

This, in a nutshell, is how our own mind controls us. We form certain beliefs in our minds, and despite becoming far stronger than these shackles, we still let them control us. The reason for this is, at some point, we simply give up trying to understand our mind and just accept that it controls us.

Here's a question for you: Have you ever looked at yourself from a third person's perspective? Have you ever examined your thoughts from a third person's perspective? If you haven't, do so now.

Freedom and Thought

Having performed that exercise, here's a follow-up question: If your mind is singular, who was doing the observation? In other words, if there is just one 'you', who was observing you? All of it was inside your head, so it's not as if someone else could crawl in there.

Who was this other entity observing you?

The Thinker and the Observer

As much as we don't like to admit it, all of us have voices in our head. We conduct arguments within them all the time when debating a decision or questioning ourselves. The truth is our mind is not a single entity. It has multiple dimensions to it. Some scientists refer to this as the conscious and subconscious mind.

However, even this definition implies that there are two parts to a single mind, and as such, I don't believe this presents the full picture. Instead, I would like to think of our minds as being divided between the thinker and the observer. The thinker is the one we're all the most familiar with.

This is the part of our mind that loves to analyze things to death and flits about worrying, jumping for joy, or simply being bored while asking, 'are we there yet?' This is a telling characteristic of the thinker. You see, the thinker refuses to exist in the present moment. The only valid times for him (I'm using this in a gender-neutral way for ease of understanding) are the past and the future.

The past is where he drives his entire identity from and leans on it to justify his existence while the future holds the promise of getting out of the present. The present is just an inconvenience between the past and the future. Many spiritual teachers refer to this as the Ego. Think about the

7

English language definition of someone egotistical. It's someone who is obsessed with maintaining a certain image of themselves, no matter what.

The thinker is the Ego's primary vehicle and uses it to justify the need for all sorts of pleasures and desires. The thinker is the one who distracts you from your work by telling you that it's boring and that spending your time hanging out with your friends is a better use of your time. It is also the one who, once you're hanging out with your friends, tells you to get yourself better friends since these ones suck.

The thinker constantly builds up your ego, and this leads you to search for scraps of attention, security, and so on. While the thinker flits between the past and the future, constantly unhappy with the present, your life is going on. Your mind, fully surrendered to the thinker, is unfocused and undisciplined. This leads to difficulties in your life, as you can imagine.

If you're with a loved one and aren't fully present, what sort of a relationship can you have with that person? Once things sour, your thinker pops up again, convincing you that you're in the right and that your past is perfect evidence of this. It's all the other person's fault. It also seeks to protect itself by causing you to grieve, which is but a way of protecting your identity from scars.

On the other hand, we have the observer. The observer is completely neutral and doesn't really care too much about the past or present. Most of us have encountered him (again, gender-neutral but using him for simplicity's sake) by mistake when the thinker became too tiresome to deal with, and we detached from it and fell into a state of observation wondering, 'What on earth is going on inside my head?'

The observer represents the promise and evidence of a higher level of evolution. You can think of it this way: The thinker is the lizard brain, and the observer is the developed brain. Most people go through their entire lives not realizing this, and it's a real tragedy.

True Nature

What is nature? You might say it's the trees and the oceans, the sun and the moon and stars. Nature, however, is as spiritual an entity as it is physical. The force that created all forms of life on this planet is something that is above everything else. People refer to this force as God or Being or The Creator, what have you. This is not a religious book, so I'll merely refer to this force as nature.

The same force that created an ant is the same one that created us. Stands to reason then, that despite the vast differences between an ant and a human being, we do share some commonalities. Nature, for whatever reason, has blessed different life forms with different levels of ability. Some animals are stronger than others; some are more intelligent than others. In short, every life form has evolved a certain way for a reason we're not aware of.

As a side note, I'm not going to get into the creation versus evolution argument. If nature and God are the same thing, surely both sides of the 'debate' are arguing the same thing in a different language?

Anyway, the reasons for nature creating animals in a certain way is unknown. All that is known is that there is some purpose behind it and all of us, as animals and nature's creations are unaware of this. It stands to reason then, that if nature has created us for some purpose, it must also have given us tools necessary to prosper? Think about it, if you build a boat, would you purposely build it so that it sinks? What sense does that make?

You can see evidence of this in the way animals behave. How does a squirrel know it needs to gather food for the winter? How does a bird know it needs to migrate? How does an orphaned lion cub learn to hunt by itself? Clearly, nature has provided every single living being on this planet with some sort of mechanism whereby which it communicates the best means forward, to meet its goals.

The observer within our mind is this connection. Does nature concern itself with the past? No, it doesn't. A plant that dies does not have its clock rewound to live again. A new plant instead takes its place. Nature relentlessly marches forward. So, does this mean it's concerned with the future?

Well, in a manner, yes. But how is the future created? By doing something in the present. Hence, it stands to reason that the present moment is what nature is most concerned with. So, in order to communicate best with nature, God, divine force, what have you, it stands to reason that the thing to do is to stay focused on the present.

By staying focused on the present moment or activity, you will receive the clearest instruction from nature as to how to proceed forward successfully. If you cloud your mind by giving precedence to the thinker's voice, you snap yourself out of the present and flit between the past and the future. Your connection to the force that gave you life is broken.

Going back to our example with the elephant at the start of this chapter: If the elephant wants to be free, what should it do? Simply look at the string, look at its own huge self and simply tug! But it doesn't. Why not? Because it's stuck in the past, believing that since it could not break free back then, it can't now. It doesn't meet its objective because it is not in connection with nature.

Your relationship with your mind is much the same. You are a prisoner of the thinker within you, and the thing to do is to break free of it.

Understanding the Observer

Here's a simple exercise for you: simply observe your thoughts without judgment or approval. Much like how you look at something you're indifferent towards, look at your own thoughts, and observe the thinker within you.

Once you do this, you begin to truly understand how difficult a task it is to engage the observer and deactivate the thinker. If you're used to meditating, you know exactly what this feels like. One minute, you're sitting there reading your internal monologue and the next you've been carted off into the past thanks to your mind tricking you into getting emotionally involved with whatever it is you're thinking of.

New Consciousness

When you repeatedly keep observing your thoughts, in other words engaging the observer within you, you will watch thoughts come and go, and rise and fall. This leads to what is known as a gap in thinking. People who meditate regularly often report experiencing this gap.

A gap occurs when there is no thought flitting through your head. For someone who isn't a monk, gaps of even a few seconds are a minor miracle, so don't beat yourself up if you don't experience this during the first sitting. The gap is the best indication that you are fully present and thus, fully in touch with nature as you are meant to be.

This doesn't mean you've lost consciousness or are unaware of what's happening around you. There is no more aware state than this. This is the state in which you are as free as you will ever be to create and to achieve everything you want. Think about how artists, writers, and even sportspeople report their greatest moments of creativity.

The word 'flow' is often associated with this sort of creation whereby people report the words or music or actions simply coming out of them and of them not being aware of triggering any of it. Flow emanates from a place of relaxation, not from a place of struggle and conscious work, as we sometimes believe mistakenly in the West.

This state of flow or no-mind, as some spiritual teachers put it, is merely the observer in you being fully engaged and the thoughts that your thinker are producing are not emotionally tugging at you. You don't derive any meaning from them and merely look at them as you would a small child who is complaining about melted ice cream.

Thus, it follows from this that the best way to nurture your observer and to get into flow is to stop taking your thoughts so seriously. Stop identifying with them emotionally and recognize the truth about what is taking place. The thinker is an emotionally needy vampire who feeds on your emotions, negative or positive. Stop feeding him.

Thought

A common question at this juncture is to ask whether this means one ought to not think at all? Are we supposed to not feel any emotion or offer any thought whatsoever? Well, not quite. Once you recognize the truth about your mind and begin to engage the observer, you will fall in line with what nature has made you be.

Every one of us has a different purpose in life, a different gift to offer. We know what this is when we're children. Think about how children behave. When children play, they wholeheartedly jump into it, getting lost in their own world, no matter what is happening around them or who is looking at them. Now imagine an adult doing the same thing. They'll earn themselves a one-way ticket to an asylum.

This illustrates the sort of pressure we put ourselves under as we grow up and disconnect from nature. Would you ever claim a child has no emotions? Far from it. As far as I can tell, children seem to be happy all the time and love everything. So why would you think you need to be an emotionless android to be present?

Being present is an intensely emotional state, one of peace, happiness, and love. It is from this base that you are free to create whatever it is you want. This is how you free yourself.

Body and Mind

If your observing mind is your connection to nature, your body is the means by which to express this connection. A person who is disconnected from nature, whether sad or happy, is often tensed in their body. Try to observe this the next time you're feeling overjoyed. You will feel every muscle in you tense up and adrenaline and dopamine flowing through you. It's a great feeling for sure.

Then observe yourself when you're sad or depressed about something. Notice how some parts of your body will be tensed, particularly the chest or back. Our emotions manifest themselves throughout our body, and there's nothing we can do to hide this.

This begs the question; if our emotions manifest in our bodies, can we change our emotions by changing our bodily state? Well, of course, we can. This is what exercise is. Think about how you feel after a great workout or a run. Physical movement will affect our minds and refresh it in the short term.

It is the mind that is in control and is your best connection to nature. Nurturing this connection is the path the happiness and self-emancipation.

A Practical Exercise

This book is not just about waxing spiritual about mind and nature. It will also give you practical exercises to do, which will help enhance your connection with nature. As we've seen, one of the ways we can determine when our thinker is in control is by observing tension within our body.

We've also seen how changing our physical reality changes our mental one. This relaxation exercise is the result of this phenomenon. In the beginning, I recommend doing this for as long as you can. A key thing to note is that you should not do this lying down or fall asleep when practicing this. Sleep is a loss of consciousness, and this is all about relaxing yourself into consciousness.

Begin by sitting on a chair with your back unsupported. Take a few deep breaths to relax. Notice how your body becomes softer with every exhale and tenses up or hardens with every inhale.

Now close your eyes and mentally walk through each part of your body from your feet to your head and then your head to your feet. Relax and release the tension in each part of your body. Next, imagine yourself as being made of stone. Extremely heavy stone.

Imagine yourself sinking into the chair, deeper and deeper. Imagine someone stops by to try and lift you and this is impossible, you're far too heavy. Rest in this state of heaviness for as long as you can.

Next, imagine yourself being deflated. The air is being let out of you, slowly and soon your whole body is flat, draped on the chair. Remain in this state for as long as you can.

Slowly open your eyes and take note of how you feel. Notice any physical tension or the lack of it.

Perform this exercise every day and build your stamina up to 15 minutes at the very least.

IT STARTS

WITH YOU

CHAPTER 2

Eliminating Stress and Empowering Yourself

E motions play an important part in our lives. On the one hand you have the positive ones of happiness, joy and so on and on the other hand we have negative ones like fear, stress, anxiety and so on. Understand this; you will never be able to stop bad things from happening in your life. Dealing with the bad along with the good is a basic fact of existence.

Too many people focus on increasing happiness and being happy all the time. There's a fundamental misunderstanding of the way the world works within you if you happen to expect this. Having such unrealistic expectations is what makes you sad in the first place. Other expectations make us sad as well and devolve into stress, anxiety, and fear.

This chapter will help you understand a fundamental fact of life: You cannot stop bad things from occurring. However, you can change your relationship with them and free yourself from their shackles.

Pain

Let's say there's a job you really want. This job will help you provide for your family and ensure your finances are strong for the rest of your life. You interview well and all signs from the manager point to the fact that you'll receive the offer. Then, one day, you receive an email saying, "Thank you for your application. We're sorry to inform you...."

This is a common scenario most people face, and it offers a good insight into how we deal with negative emotions. Can you force someone to hire you? You can't. Is it OK to feel sad at the fact that you didn't receive the job you wanted? Yes, of course. Are you justified in taking this sadness and relating it to you past and blowing it out of proportion in your head? No, you're not and this is where the problem begins.

Things do not acquire meaning in and as of themselves. All meaning that they acquire comes from your method of labelling them. If everyone one day, collectively decided gold is as valuable as stone, how do you think you'll view gold?

The Ego and Fear

The reason your mind jumps and rushes to label your disappointment and to create some bigger meaning out of it is because your thinker is fully in charge. Remember, the thinker within you is simply acting out of a need to protect your ego. You see, the ego is an emotional vampire.

What I mean by this is, the ego and the thinker need constant emotional fuel to keep burning. It takes energy to flit between the past and the future, and this must come from somewhere! The thinker revels in creating situations that cause emotional drama. You'll often see people creating friction deliberately in their relationships. Why do you think this is?

Aiming to be happy and to only focus on things that make you happy is a clever way we get tricked by the thinker into providing it with fuel. A basic fact of the ego is that it is insatiable and adjusts to novelty very easily. A good example of this is when you receive a present that you really like. When it's brand new and shiny, you love it and are the happiest person in the world.

A year later, once you're used to it, what next? You need something else. People who focus on and try to be happy all the time reduce this period of satisfaction that they feel when they acquire something that makes them happy. The ego craves more and more happiness, and eventually, no amount of it can satisfy it anymore. What happens then? You feel sad.

You see, the ego was not feeding on happiness at all. It was getting you to feel sad and was damaging your relationship with things that make you happy. This is exactly the process by which people come to associate pleasure with pain. If pursuing happiness results in pain, then the thinker reasons that pain equals pleasure. Next thing you know, you're sabotaging all chances of happiness and becoming a glutton for punishment.

All of this doesn't play out consciously. What I mean is, you will not be aware of your actions of sabotage as you're carrying them out. How can you be? You're firmly in the thinker's grasp. The thing you must understand above all else is the nature of the ego and its insatiable need for emotion.

Once you understand this, you're ready to proceed to the next step which will help you deal with negativity correctly.

Shining a Light

If pain and negativity within yourself can be thought of as darkness, then awareness and presence can be thought of as the light. How does one dispel darkness? It is not done by fighting it or banishing it. You simply need to switch on the light. In the same manner, awareness of the present moment confuses the ego and its henchman, the thinker.

The ego requires the foundation of time to function properly. The past and the future are what give the ego meaning. The past and the future constructs are fixed as far as the ego is concerned. Once it has this stability, timewise, it is free to sit down and draw meaning and emotion out of it to feed itself.

The present, by contrast, is not fixed as far as time is concerned. It is forever changing and is moving. It is always 'now'. It is fluid. There is nothing for the ego or the thinker to latch onto to derive meaning. Even when something bad occurs in the present moment, say you receive the letter declining your application, the first thing the thinker does is take you to the future or to the past.

You might be forced to relive prior rejection, which was painful or visualize a future where nothing is right for you. This, in turn, gives rise to fear and anxiety, ideal food for the ego. Mission accomplished, as far as the thinker is concerned. Contrasting this behavior with that of a wild animal is instructive.

When faced with a predator in the vicinity, a deer's alarm bells go off, and it instantly switches to survival mode. However, if there are no predators around, do you think a deer suffers from any anxiety or fear? No, it simply keeps munching grass and doing whatever deer do when they aren't eating or sleeping.

The deer is constantly in the present moment. Animals and other life forms do not have a concept of time, which is solely a manmade construct. To them, time is always 'now'. Does this mean we should abandon progress and turn back to living in the wild? Well, not quite.

Imagination

When creating man, nature has provided us with a powerful double-edged sword in the form of our mind. More than any other creature, man has the ability to create reality. Thus far, the thinker within our mind has been cast as the villain, doing the ego's bidding, and plotting against us in order to generate as much emotional drama as possible. However, this is simply because we haven't truly realized the full purpose of the thinker.

Nature does not create or provide for without reason. You see, the thinker is merely an outlet for our imagination. When misdirected, the thinker imagines nightmare scenarios and builds the ego. You can think of the ego as simply being the negative manifestation of untapped potential within a person. The more a person shies away from their purpose and removes themselves from nature, the greater their ego.

Put it another way: Happy and fulfilled people do not have egos. It is those who realize they have lived unfulfilled lives that have egos the size of the planet.

Setting the Thinker Straight

While most of your thoughts should be engaging the observer, that is, simply living in the moment by observing things as they come and go and reacting to things happening in the moment, you should not aim to silence the thinker. The thinker has enormous ability when it comes to shining a light on the darkness within you.

Let us step back and understand how worry and anxiety unfold. A trigger occurs in your immediate environment, and this causes you to relive past situations which match the current trigger. This leads you to relive the painful moment in your head. Next, your mind jumps forward into the future and paints scenarios, which are unfavorable. These in turn trigger emotions within you, which lead to more pictures and so on.

What is really happening here? You imagine scenarios in your head on the basis of certain emotional triggers. The key word being imagining. Those pictures are real enough to cause you worry and pain. What if instead of creating negative pictures, you could create positive ones instead? Just like how imagined negative pictures create negative emotions, could you create positive emotion by imagining positive pictures. Absolutely!

This is what the process of visualization is all about. Your observer cannot do this for you, but the thinker is a master of this. For many people, the thinker's thermostat is set to the negative by default and thanks to a lack of training, it runs wild and causes a build-up of ego. If, however, you were to direct it positively and in the right amounts, you will be able to create a life for yourself exactly as you want it.

A deer or other lower life forms do not have this ability to imagine. They don't have the thinker within them, just the observer. While this helps them in many ways, ultimately all a deer does is survive. Man has the ability to do so much more than that. The degree to which you 'live' is determined by how efficiently you deploy your thinker.

The majority of your time should still be devoted to the observer. However, feel free to indulge in mental imagery, which makes you feel good and in which you imagine achieving all the things you want. There is a trap here of starting to covet the things you imagine.

The best way of describing the tone your thoughts should take is to ask the question, "wouldn't it be great if....?" For example, after your interview, you think to yourself "wouldn't it be great if I got this job? I would love the higher salary it offers." That's it. You don't rush ahead by thinking, "I have the job, and now I'm going to get everything I want." Once your thought is done, you simply get back to your observer and let nature take its course.

The funny thing is, when you do this, you'll automatically find nature giving you all the things you want. The reason for this is because you're more in touch with nature via this process and your mind is not clouded with negativity. Thanks to this connection, nature will provide the means for you to achieve your goals, and you'll be in full receiving mode to interpret these signs.

The Self

The act of engaging your observer is a powerful means of getting outside of yourself. When observing, you don't have time to make any judgment or recall painful memories. Things just are. This leads you to recognize that there is a power and reason greater than yours, that is nature.

Recalling what we learned previously, nature is the one that has created you and has done so with the express intention to help you succeed. Thus, if you're closer to nature, how could you possibly fail? The importance of 'you' melts in the face of this argument since if you don't have to worry about yourself, you have no reason to recognize the existence of 'you.'

This doesn't mean to say you can throw yourself in front of a bus and expect nature to help you out of its path. That is just being silly. The point is, you will begin to trust that nature has provided with ample means and tools for you to achieve what you want and create everything that you desire. What's more, it is even willing to give you detailed directions and instruction manuals as to how to go about creating it.

All you need to do in return is to listen. This is so simple it's mind-boggling to most people. Yet, we see evidence of this every day all around us. We innately understand the need to protect things we create and to ensure that they can prosper. We can see evidence of nature guiding living beings by observing the behavior of animals that do not have advanced thought capabilities.

We can see how our world operates on a higher level of intelligence than we are capable of understanding. All we thus, need to do is get closer to nature. We do this by asking, via the thinker, for what we want, and then getting back to observing nature for that is where the keys and clues to achieve what we want are embedded.

The Key to Defeat Anxiety

There are two forms of fear. One is the natural reaction to a threat in the present, which is completely normal and legitimate. The other is a psychological reaction to something perceived in the future. In other words, one is real, and the other is imagined. When our minds have galloped into the future, we physically remain in the here and now.

This inability to move forward coupled with the perceived desire to know what happens creates a vicious gap which manifests itself as anxiety. If fear is present in the current moment, we can immediately and usually do, act on it. Thus, there is no chance for anxiety to be formed. The vicious gap, however, needs to express itself somehow, and anxiety is the prime emotion for it to do so.

Working backward from this, all the trouble seems to be when our minds decide to run away into the future. Why is this? It's because our thinker is not trained yet and is like a wild animal of immense power. Every so often he runs in the right direction, and we benefit immensely, but when he runs in unpredictable patterns, we suffer.

The act of staying firmly in the present and using the thinker to just ask for what we want and then getting back to observing is akin to training a wild animal to obey our commands. Much like a wild animal that is used to getting its way, it will fight back viciously and will resist. With persistence, though, you will get it to channel its power in the right direction.

The Self Image

People who suffer from anxiety and general negativity usually have an image of themselves as being 'this way' onto their minds. Their thinker has been trained to produce only these kinds of images, and as a result, their ego grows. The ego, in turn, demands even more emotion to sustain itself and this negative self-image, the prime generator of emotion, becomes even stronger.

How does one rectify this image? Well, it begins with knowledge. We've already seen how every living being has been created with the express purpose of succeeding in this world. The tools and instruction manuals have also been given. Therefore, it stands to reason that the only reason you have not received what you want is because you simply haven't been listening.

If this is true, how can your self-image of being an anxiety-ridden, failure-prone person be possibly true? It doesn't add up.

Knowing something is half the battle. The next step is to reinforce it. The thinker is a spoiled wild animal. He is used to doing whatever he wants because you have not been controlling him enough. The time is now. Start observing the manifestations of nature all around you. Notice how every living being is given tools to succeed by nature. Notice how people seem to create best when their conscious minds are switched off.

Read accounts of athletes and sports persons being in the zone, and you'll realize what they're describing is a connection with nature. Start engaging your observer and use the observer to look at how childish and petulant the thinker can be. Marvel at the tool that has been given to you by nature and pat yourself on the back for finally beginning to use it the right way.

As you do this, you'll see the anxiety that is caused by the vicious gap simply melt away and be replaced by stable, peaceful happiness.

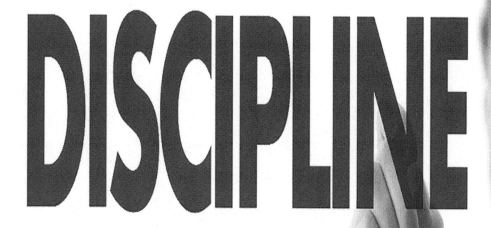

CHAPTER 3

Understanding Your Existence

Many philosophers over the years have debated the reason for the existence of life. What purpose does it serve? Who is served by this purpose, whatever it is? Modern western philosophy tends to take a jaundiced view of life's purpose in general. Reasoning backward from the fact that there doesn't seem to be an apparent purpose, we can deduce that life, in and as of itself, is without purpose and is, therefore, trivial.

Hence, all our actions and beliefs during our lifetimes are trivial and are inconsequential. In short, nothing matters very much. The problem with this line of thought is that it makes just enough sense to seem plausible and then takes a wrong turn, thereby arriving at a nonsensical conclusion.

Ancient eastern philosophy starts off with the same reasoning but usually arrives at a very different, in fact opposite, outcome.

Zen and You

Ancient eastern philosophies such as Buddhism and Hinduism don't concern themselves too much about proving themselves right. This is because the original premise they begin with is that there is some greater purpose which human beings do not understand, and that's perfectly OK. The primacy of human intelligence and existence is assumed as a given in western thought, and this leads to some conflicting conclusions.

This chapter isn't about comparing philosophies. Instead, what we will aim to do is to understand how these trains of thought can be adapted in a practical manner to benefit our lives. The human condition is complex. The path to understanding doesn't lie in the debate, but via traveling within. If this inward journey brings even a modicum of understanding about the true nature of things, its benefit can be measured in lifetimes.

Zen Buddhism and practice offers a good summation of how you can adopt these philosophies into your daily life. Before we get into any practice, though, it is essential to understand the spirit upon which it is built.

The Spirit of Zen

Like all Buddhist philosophy, Zen's aim is to attain enlightenment. What is enlightenment? Enlightenment is a condition whereby a soul is not reborn into the world. Buddhist philosophy assumes that all lives are reincarnated and your form in the next life depends on the level of enlightenment in your previous.

Substitute the word enlightenment for evolution, and this begins to make things a bit clearer. According to Buddhist principles, the purpose of all life is to attain a higher level of evolution. Therefore, one might assume a particularly industrious ant might be reborn as a bird and so on and so forth.

While the scientific veracity of this is in doubt, as human beings, it does give us a nice framework within which to live.

If the true purpose of life is to discover enlightenment, the thing to do is to follow the basic principles to discover it. Notice, enlightenment is defined as learning the truth about the nature of life. What is the truth? Well, this is for you to discover since the truth at your stage of evolution will be different from someone else's.

This means the path to enlightenment lies by discovering yourself. The basic premise of Zen is that every human being born has the seed of enlightenment within them. This gets hidden, however, as we go through life and build layers upon layers of the ego on top of it. The thing to do is to let go of the ego and rediscover that initial seed.

Practicing the path of enlightenment with the intention of discovering it is only feeding the ego. You see, it's not the outcome that matters, but the path. You need to stay focused on the path you're taking and understand that right action leads to the right outcome. In other words, stay focused on the present and let yourself be guided by right action. The key word in all of this being 'let.'

You cannot consciously create a path for yourself since you don't know what the future is going to being. Therefore, you need to relax in the present and allow the path to come to you. Contrast this philosophy with what was discussed in the previous chapter about engaging the observer within and letting nature give us signals and us reacting in the present. It's the exact same idea, expressed in different terms.

Therefore, if the purpose of life is to attain enlightenment, and the way to attain enlightenment is to practice remaining in the present and practicing right action in the moment, it follows that the purpose of life is to practice acting correctly by staying in the present moment. Stay in the present, and nature will bring your path to you and all you need to do is to follow it.

There are some additional principles which will aid our quest to stay in the present moment. Incorrect understanding of them might throw us off the path, so it's essential to grasp these concepts.

Transiency

One of the foundational truths of our existence is the fact that everything changes. Whether the change is for good or for bad, the fact remains that change comes for everyone. The greater the resistance to change, the larger the suffering we will undergo. An important lesson about the nature of the self or "I" can be derived from this.

If everything is changing all the time, you are changing as well. If you keep changing all the time, how can you ever define or nail down what "you" or "I" are? The truth is that the nature of yourself is in constant flux. The sooner you accept this truth, the easier life becomes.

Accepting that things always change also helps us understand that good and bad are transient things. Something that is bad can lead to good and vice versa. If your life is good right now, no matter, the change will soon come, and things might turn bad or a different degree of good. This sounds fatalistic, but if you dig into this, the real teaching here is that it isn't our place to worry about what sort of change will come.

If your reaction to reading the previous sentences was one of sadness or some negative emotion, then you're worried about the future and about what changes will happen in your life. This is the ego taking you out of the present moment. The real lesson in this principle is to understand that change will come constantly. So, our job is to simply live in the present to make the best of this current moment.

Think of it this way: Let's say you're on a journey, driving to a place 100 miles away. As you drive, you know the scenery will change and that eventually, you'll arrive at your destination and that you'll eventually stop driving. Do you sit there worrying about when you'll stop driving? Would you worry about what you'll do when you stop driving? Would you worry about what sort of trees you might see along the way? I should think not!

The difficulty of staying in the present, via an imperfect understanding of transience, can be illustrated by the same example. Let's say you're driving there for an important job interview. Well, the stakes are higher now. Maintaining a neutral stance towards your arrival time is a far tougher task. Some people might interpret this, incorrectly, as thinking they shouldn't care about the arrival time and just do what they want.

Well, this is where western philosophy veers off the track as well. The key word here is not indifference but equanimity. You prepare to get there on time and control what you can. Beyond that, relax and let nature take you there. On the outside, both states seem similar, but in terms of intention, it's a different universe altogether.

Embrace the truth of transience and more importantly, practice it in your life by staying the present. You'll find your quality of life improves.

Mindfulness and Emptiness

A key to living well in the present moment is to empty our minds. This doesn't mean you forget everything you've learned and make your brain an empty slate. Instead, the correct way of presenting yourself is to have a soft brain; in other words, one which is ready to absorb change. Change comes in the form of opposing views and challenges to your thought as well.

Examining recent political discourse provides an excellent lesson in how not to have a brain ready to absorb change. The shrill nature of debate and the black or white presentation of things shows an unwillingness to accept change and to be ready to deal with it. Emptying your brain of such preconceived notions and being willing to accept the fact that opposing views exist will reduce your suffering.

The emptiness of your mind will also bring about mindfulness. Mindfulness has become something of a craze this past decade with everyone preaching it as a path to enlightenment. However, practicing or trying to practice it without emptying your mind is a futile exercise. You won't have space in your mind to observe anything if it's already full of something else.

Mindfulness is simply concentration, and single intentioned thought practiced in the present. Your brain is at its most powerful and receptive to nature when it is focused on the task at hand and firmly in the present. This way, you are in pole position to receive nature's blessings and improve your life in magical ways.

An important point to note here with regards to emptiness is that you shouldn't empty your mind of all your hopes and dreams. As mentioned earlier, adopting a tone of "wouldn't it be nice if....." is the perfect way to ask or wish for things because it provides room for the receipt of something better and recognition of the fact that we don't always know what's best for ourselves.

It's perfectly fine to wish for improvement in life. This is, after all your purpose in life, as we saw in the previous sections. Your thinker will help you form the picture of what you want, and your observer will help you stay tuned to the present to receive nature's guidance as to how to get there. The key is to avoid becoming welded to your dream or hardening your mind by saying, "I want nothing else, but…." This is an imperfect understanding and is prime material for your ego to jump in and throw you off track.

When you're solid in your thought, you cannot be present. A soft, accepting state of mind is ideal for bringing about greater levels of calmness.

Attachment

This is a particularly difficult point to grasp for a lot of people. The very nature of human existence puts a huge emphasis on the nature of "I." In other words, "I" comes before everything else. Everyone wants a better life, a better house, better clothes, cars and so on. One might even think this sort of pursuit is right in line with the idea of bettering ourselves.

Well, bettering yourself means understanding the truth about existence and living in acceptance or harmony with it. Chasing after shiny things, as your sole purpose, is contrary to all of this since placing anything on a pedestal is living in ignorance of the transient nature of things.

Material objects are not the only things people covet. Intelligence and wisdom are another quality a lot of people are attached to. "I'm more intelligent than he/she is, therefore, I'm better" is a typical thought a lot of us have. This sort of thinking is hardly the hallmark of an empty mind, ready to receive knowledge from nature.

Who is to say who is wise and who is mad? You might have heard this story previously: Once upon a time, there was a town whose inhabitants were the most learned in the world. The town was synonymous with prosperity, peace, and everything good you can imagine. The rest of the world looked to the town for cues on everything and followed its cues since its stature was so high.

Well, one day an inhabitant of the town contracted a disease. This was a terrible disease which drove her mad and caused her to behave in ways which no one understood or could comprehend. The rest of the townsfolk placed her in an asylum, the first ever built, and carried on. However, the disease was contagious. Soon, more and more people started going crazy, and the asylum began filling up. Eventually, the entire town went mad and the rest of the world with it.

All except for one man. He was somehow immune to this disease and remained sane. Unfortunately, the town and the rest of the world now thought he was the insane one and promptly threw him into the asylum.

Who is wise, and who is the fool? Who knows? Perhaps the way forward in all of this is to recognize that attachment to a particular idea or quality within ourselves, the "I," is a form of madness.

Practice

The idea behind all the material presented in this book is for you to go ahead and practice it. The trouble with the sort of material presented in this book is that all of it is very satisfying to discuss and engage with intellectually. There is a temptation to compare it to other forms of thought and to write papers on it.

Well, doing just this is betraying a complete misunderstanding of what is being communicated. The idea behind all of this is for you to go out and practice. You need to engage emotionally with these principles and discover your way forward. Without this, there is no progress and thus, no peace.

There are exercises presented throughout this book for you to practice. While it is ideal for you to do all of them, performing at least one of them will help your progress towards your goals and build your discipline, by providing structure to your day.

We've already looked at a relaxation exercise for you to do. Now, we will look at an exercise which will help you train your thinker to work for you and aid the observer. This is a two-part exercise. At first, it's a good idea to aim for five minutes of each, and then build the total practice time up to 30 minutes per session, divided into two sessions of fifteen.

Seat yourself on the floor, cross-legged or on a chair with your back unsupported and begin by taking a few deep breaths. Ideally, you'll perform the relaxation exercise prior to this, but this isn't a hard and fast rule. As you notice yourself relax, close your eyes, and pay attention to any sounds in your vicinity. How loud they are, whether they repeat or occur just one.

Also notice the contact your physical form is making with other objects outside of you. If you're on the floor, notice how your feet feel against the floor or carpet. If on the chair, notice the friction between your legs and the floor and the seat. Notice how it feels. Now gently, draw your attention towards your breath. Notice the inhalation and the exhalation.

Do not count or chant anything in your head as you do this simply observe. Whether it's fast or slow, deep or heavy, whatever it is, let it be as it is and simply observe it. Now try to observe which nostril you're inhaling and exhaling from. Usually, one nostril is blocked, and the other is open, with both nostril switching roles every few hours.

Notice how cool the inhaled breath feels and how warm the exhaled breath is. Notice the speed differences, if any, between the two. Your mind will wander in between all of this. Gently bring it back to your breathing, without any admonishment or judgment, and start observing again.

The second part of this exercise is to engage your thinker. Your observer has you nice and relaxed, and this is the best moment to get the thinker fired up. What are some of the things you want in your life? There is no guilt in asking for the things you desire, so don't feel shy. Visualize this in your mind, as clearly as you can, and draw a picture.

A lot of people will find they can't form a clear picture at first, but this will get better with practice. Engage and play around with the idea of having it. How do you feel now that this thing is in your life? Focus on how happy you feel. Notice how the energy in your body builds up and that sitting silently on the floor becomes more and more difficult. You will feel the need to jump up and down, out of excitement, perhaps.

Are you smiling yet? How does your breath feel? Continue observing as many details as you can, for as long as you can. In the beginning, your mind will get exhausted soon but keep practicing, and you'll soon want to do multiple sessions of this practice.

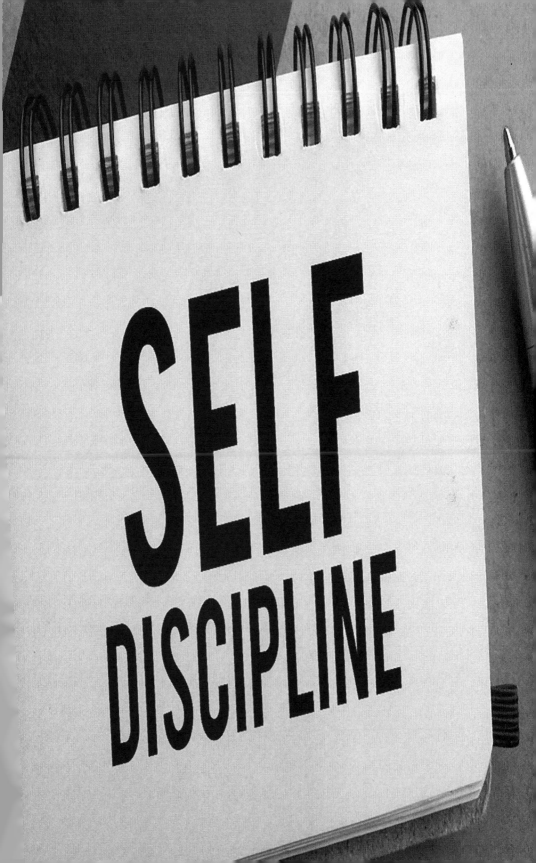

CHAPTER 4

The Tyranny of Time

Time, that eternal obsession of the human mind. We place a huge deal of importance on our ability to follow the clock and on never being late. So much of our day is ruled by the clock, to the extent that when we feel hungry, we check to clock to see whether it is an appropriate time to eat!

Understand that there are two forms of time. Regular time is simply what is displayed on your watch. This is the time that helps us stay on track in terms of appointments and letting us know what time of the day it is. Then there's irregular time. This time manifests itself as pressure. "I'm 30 years old, and I'm broke." This is the time that is born out of an obsession with the past or the future.

In short, it is born out of the ego. In this chapter, we'll dig into the true nature of time and how to make it work for you instead of the other way around. You will see that to the extent that time causes disquiet within you, that is the extent of your attachment with your "I."

The Nature of Time

An obsession with time is simply the ego trying to satisfy itself by forming an identity to hang on to. By harking back to the past, or rushing into the future, the ego is doing its best to generate some emotion to feed itself. An example of this is the "I'm X years old, and I haven't done Y yet" fallacy.

This illusionary need to have achieved something by a certain point is simply the ego using your attachment to your "I" to terrorize you. Some people will argue that this is a form of motivation and gets people to stop being lazy and achieve something.

Well, a counterargument is, if a person is focused on the now, surely, they would recognize the reality of their current situation and work to rectify things since it is in every living being's nature to work towards bettering its lot. So, what is the need to harm yourself by conjuring scary visions of time?

Another argument is: Isn't the process of visualization using time to make ourselves feel better? If time is not real, then why should one visualize? This is an excellent question, and the answer helps us understand the nature of the present moment better.

Time and Now

When working towards achieving some goal, a key point to recognize is that achieving the goal depends on our execution of a series of 'now' moments. In other words, the journey is where you will be spending the majority of your time. Every goal begins with a visualization, which is a projection of the future.

This projection certainly makes you feel good. However, it doesn't feed your ego because, in order to execute your vision correctly, you need to execute the steps that will take you there. If you spend the entirety of your time only visualizing and not doing, you're feeding your ego. By proceeding to 'do,' you're snapping yourself out of the future and simply executing in the now.

Indeed, your ability to reach your goal is dictated by your ability to be as present as possible. Thus, the question arises, what is the best time for you to do anything? It's now! What time is it most of the time? Now! Time, in terms of speaking of the past and the future, is a delusion. The past did happen, yes, but those moments have gone and are a series of previous nows.

They have no bearing on what you need to do in the current now. What you need to do in the present moment is dictated by where you want to go, that is the future you wish to create for yourself. Since creating this depends on your actions in the present, surely it follows that the best time to focus on is the present.

Thus, as you can see, time is an illusion. The past is irrelevant, and the future is yet to be created by your actions in the present. Fully focusing your energy on your current task is what brings you closer to nature and your goal. Living in the past or in the future is to oscillate between feelings of regret and anticipation.

You'll be a pendulum incessantly moving back and forth while your present moments keep slipping by you. As a result, you end up creating even more painful pasts and even more anticipatory futures, and your ego's appetite grows and grows until one day, you simply cannot take it anymore.

Communication from Nature

Nature cannot communicate to you in the future or in the past. This is because, right now, they don't exist! Only now exists. Conditions such as stress, anxiety, and depression are a result of oscillating back and forth and refusing to stay present. Meditation and mindfulness are great techniques to force yourself to remain present.

A lot of people who suffer from depression though do not see the benefits that meditation can provide because they use it incorrectly. You see, people flit back and forth in the first place because they find their current conditions intolerable. As a reflex, they move back and forth to cope with the current pain.

However, as we have seen, this only builds pain. Mediation, by forcing them to become more present, initially magnifies the pain by casting a spotlight on it. A lot of people instinctively fear this spotlight and are afraid of their ability to cope. Thus, at the slightest sign of pain, they seek to escape.

The reality is that while the initial moments will be painful, you will soon observe that the pain is usually coming from an attachment to the past of the future, not the present. Even the pain that is caused in the present is caused by an attachment to the notion of self or the "I." Shining the light of awareness on these causes will cause you to understand the source of your pain and, as every living being is engineered to do so, you will seek to rectify your situation automatically.

The means to rectify it will come to you from nature in the present moment. All of this is easier said than done, of course, but remember what we learned in the previous chapter. The practice itself is enlightenment. Regular, determined, and deliberate practice is how you engineer and create a better life from your current pain. This is what ancient philosophers, including the Buddha, speak of when they say, "there is good even in pain."

Accessing True Power

When you move out of the past or the future and fully into the present, you will be able to access the full power of your mind. This is because your mind, which is but an extension of nature, works best in the present moment, where nature actually exists. By falling into the ego trap and getting emotionally involved with the past of the future, we unplug ourselves from our greatest source of power.

If there is a fault within us as human beings, it is that we tend to direct our attention to whatever is making the most noise. This can be observed in small children when they don't get what they want; they soon learn to cry and make a scene until they do receive their wish. The thinker within us is like this child.

When undisciplined, he is loud and untrained. As a result, he kicks up such a big row that eventually we're forced to turn our untrained attention to him, and the thinker happily takes us along for a ride. The observer, meanwhile, quiet as ever, goes by unnoticed.

The key to breaking free and making sure you remain in the present, now, the moment is to stop identifying with the thinker. The thinker isn't 'you.' You are the master of the thinker and the observer and have the power to engage both parts of your mind, as and when you please. You have the ability and the discipline within you to do so.

A lot of people identify with their thinker, believing this to be the full representation of their minds. People who are academically intelligent fall prey to this more than most. As a result, they only end up learning things within books and forget that an entire body of knowledge exists if they only looked up from their books.

The thinker has no use for observation or the present since it revels in making things up. As mentioned before, you need to harness this energy and direct it towards your own greater good. Much like loving parents who realize their child is acting spoiled by protesting in a shrill manner all the time, you need to teach and enforce discipline on your thinker. In the same way that the discipline is good for the child, your thinker will appreciate and reward you for it.

Letting Go of Pain

A common stumbling block people will face when starting to identify the now is to look at it from a theoretical and scientific perspective. What this means is, most will understand the now moment as being the one holding 'true facts.' This does not mean to say that science and theory are bad; far from it. But everything has its time and place.

Looking at the present moment from this understanding or perspective is to simply fall into the ego's trap once again. The ego can easily convince you that the past is also a collection of facts and the next thing you know, you're reliving your worst nightmares, only this time, via the prism of 'facts.'

People who are suffering from a lot of emotional pain in their lives, when they work towards being present, often complain that the present is too full of pain, and it makes them feel worse. The mental pattern described above is what is causing this. You see, pain is merely a function of time. Guilt, anxiety, stress, fear, and the like are simply caused by being too focused on the past and not on the present.

A good question to ask yourself is this: What is a problem I'm facing right now? The answer will usually pop into your head. What can you do about it right now? The answer will again pop into your head. It is at this point that people derail themselves by engaging the thinker. It comes rushing in and starts creating images of how life would be once the solution is implemented. This leads to a rush of good feelings.

Then, just as suddenly, the nice pictures vanish because we realize we're not in the future yet, but in the present where the problem still persists. This causes us to feel bad, and we fall into the vicious circle again. Do you see how your attachment to time is causing you pain? Are you aware of it?

If, after being presented with a solution, you simply moved forward and began implementing steps to put it in place, you would actually be doing something to brighten your future. The key to your future is your present. This is a fact that we understand intellectually but fail to grasp emotionally since we engage the thinker far too much.

You Are Not Your Current Condition

After making a mistake, how many of you have said, "Oh no, I broke the glass"? How many of you have said, "Oh no, I'm such a klutz"? While breaking a vase or some such thing might not seem important, if we're on an emotional cliff of sorts, this tiny mistake can push us over the edge.

One of the reasons as to why we even find ourselves on the cliff's edge, in the first place, is because of emotional involvement with the problem or a mistake. We tend to adopt the mistake as an innate quality of ourselves. If you wish to free yourself from your pain, it is not enough to merely move into the present but to also detach yourself from the need to label yourself.

If you've been paying attention thus far, you'll see that this is nothing more than letting go of the need for an "I." Why do people want an "I" in the first place? The need usually springs from the insecurity of simply remaining present. It feels like a void and people, not knowing that the observer is the one who helps us stay in the present, engage the thinker instead, and he ends up doing what he does best, create images to soothe us.

Learn to separate your need for identity from your current life situation. Instead of saying "I'm such a klutz" simply think "I made a mistake. I'll seek to rectify it." Notice the difference between those two observations and notice which part of your mind is making those observations. Needless to say, it should be obvious which one is better for your overall freedom and peace.

Achieving Goals

You might be wondering, if time is an illusion, isn't goal setting an illusion as well? You're correct it is. However, to understand the nature of goal setting and ambition, this is the incorrect question to ask. As mentioned before, human beings have a thinker within us who can assist us in achieving things which aren't in existence yet.

One of the keys to getting the thinker to work for us, instead of against us, is to let go of time. However, if the act of drawing pictures in the future is using time, then how is one supposed to do this? Well, this dilemma usually indicates an imperfect understanding of the difference between regular and irregular time.

Remember, we looked at this in the introduction to this chapter. Irregular time is the one that brings about psychological pressure and is firmly disconnected from the present moment. Using time in tandem with the present moment is to draw a picture in our minds, using the thinker, and the recognizing the steps we need to execute to get there and working on it in the present.

How does one aid his process? Well, letting go of your need for an "I" is the key to all this. Why does your thinker even feel the need to go back and forth, between past and future? It's because of your need for an identity, a need to define yourself. The present moment is ever changing and fluid and those of us that cannot accept its nature, find ourselves jumping to a future or a past that is fixed, non-changing, and comfortable.

Even those who suffer from immense amounts of pain are doing this to put themselves at ease. The fear that the lack of acceptance of the present moment's true nature brings is far many magnitudes greater than the pain that the past stores. Thus, the past is a more manageable situation than the present, and people get stuck in it.

If you let go of the need for an "I," you will not feel the need jump back and forth, you will not feel the need to make every situation about you and to constantly pass judgment about the world or yourself. You will simply exist. In turn, by simply existing, you will be bet placed, with a clear mind to observe what is happening around you and turn it to your advantage.

Therefore, more than reading about all this, practicing is essential. Remember, enlightenment lies in practice, not in simply reading and debating. Practice is following all these principles, and even a minute's worth of practice is far more beneficial than reading this book a million times over.

CHAPTER 5

Mental Traps to Beware of

Your mind is not a dumb being. As you look to change your outlook on things, it will, inevitably, fight back. You must understand that this fight back happens not because the mind is a traitor, but as we saw in the previous chapter, it is more like an undisciplined child. You haven't given it proper direction all this while, and now, you cannot expect it to change course suddenly.

The methods the mind uses to fight back are a testament to its immense strength and the promise it holds for you when you manage to get it focused on working towards your goals and existence, as opposed to against. The first reaction will usually be one of rage. The mind will outright try to reject all change, and you will feel a great unease as you try to implement a change.

Like all anger, though, this takes a lot of energy to sustain, and this is where the mind gets creative. It lures you into traps by tricking you into thinking you are changing it when it is merely using the new ideas as a means to enforce the old ones. In this chapter, we'll take a look at some of the common ways in which the mind deceives us.

Mind Tricks

A key principle you must understand is the power of awareness. As we saw earlier, simply shining the light on ignorance is more than enough to effect a change. If you find yourself becoming more aware of these shortcomings or traps, consider it a major victory. Why? Because this is an indication that your observer is being engaged and that you're in greater communication with the present.

Acceptance…and Nothing Else

A point being hammered in this book so far is that you must accept the present for what it is and then move forward, as appropriate. The mind, via the thinker, will often come up with creative ways to achieve this without making much of a change. It will begin to cloak its efforts under the overall garb of acceptance but will resist moving forward, tricking you into thinking that acceptance is all that is required.

You see, acceptance is but the first step. It isn't enough to just accept that your current condition is not ideal, even if you begin to work to rectify it. If you've been going through a lot of pain and are at a low point in life, then acceptance will come as a huge relief. However, you cannot just stay there.

What this means is, you must relentlessly continue to dig into the nature of the present moment, constantly working to uncover your connection to nature. Once the connection is discovered in full, you will experience true joy and satisfaction. You will recognize how you're but an extension of nature and that everything is one.

If everything is the same, then there cannot be an "I" can there? This is the final step to renouncing yourself. Reaching this step is one of the hallmarks of enlightenment, and it isn't something most people achieve within a lifetime. However, remember that enlightenment is not about the goal. It is about the journey. By simply journeying forth, you are enlightened.

A person who gets stuck at simply the acceptance stage is someone who has stopped their journey. You should strive to better yourself and recognizing that there are far better states beyond acceptance is the key. Many times, the depths of pain you have experienced places a barrier to moving forward. The relief from moving out of its depths feels so good that you decide to relax right where you are.

One of the keys to moving forward is to drop your pain. So how do you drop pain? Well, how would you drop something that pricks you? You let it go. You don't need it to define you. Recognize that you are holding on to it because of a need to differentiate yourself from the rest of nature and that this is your ego acting.

The Present as a Means to the Future

A promising future depends on the present. Therefore, one must fully focus on the present to create a great future, right? Hence, correct action in the present is the key to a great future. This is a very common trap that you will almost certainly run into as you begin your journey into discovering the present.

Using and even acknowledging that the future exists is to fall into the trap of thinking irregular time exists. This trap is one that those suffering from intense pain in the present fall into, without even realizing it. The present moment is timeless and ever-changing, and this is a major threat to your ego which needs a sense of identity to survive.

In the name of progress, it tricks you into framing the acceptance of the present moment as a means to a better future and thus, a better identity. Ironically, this condition exists because of an intense attachment to the past.

Attachment need not indicate just happiness, as we normally refer to it in our daily lives. In this case, the attachment can be born out of pain as well. If the pain is intense enough and if we've struggled against it, it becomes fertile ground for our ego to carve out an identity for itself. Thus, armed with an identity that is rooted in the past and the promise of a better identity in the future, your ego justifies the present as merely something to get through.

Needless to say, nature does not work in this manner. With your mind constantly stuck in the past and the future, there's no room for anything else to get in there. Your observer is shunted off to the side where it is unable to receive any wisdom from nature. Any person who thinks that the end justifies the means in the present is a victim of this sort of thinking and is a perfect exhibit of the madness of believing in irregular time.

The thing to do is to burn the past. Simply refuse to recognize its existence beyond when it serves to teach you a lesson for a present moment. Anything other than that is dead to you, and you are dead to it. Doing this will weaken the hold a better future has on you, and you will begin to recognize the present for what it truly is.

Waiting

The law of attraction is something that has become immensely popular during this millennium, and the number of books describing this effect has quadrupled. Almost every one of these books focuses on the asking part but don't make any mention of the next step, that is, the action.

The process, according to the books, usually goes like this. You feel an intense desire for something you want and ask the universe for it. The universe will eventually give this to you because it loves you. The veracity of this is not in dispute. However, the process, as described above, will lead those with an imperfect understanding of the way nature works, astray.

Nature will always work to support you because you are a creation of it. As mentioned earlier, would you ever consider destroying or deliberately engineering something you create to fail? Our nature and instincts are the same as the universal nature, and this is proof of the fact that every living being has been equipped for success.

Thus, asking the universe or nature for what you desire is likely to result in you receiving it. The trap that people fall into is to then simply start waiting, instead of focusing on the present and taking cues from nature. People who do this expect to receive the object of their desire in its full form and exactly as they think it ought to arrive.

One is reminded of the joke where there's a man drowning in a lake. He prays intensely to God for rescue, and soon a boat turns up offering help. The man declines, saying God will rescue him! Those who merely wait for the thing they ask for to arrive are victims of the same sort of thinking as the misbegotten man in the joke.

Nature will give you not the thing you desire, but the opportunity to walk the path to the thing you desire. You still need to get up and walk. Nature will not do the work for you. This sort of waiting is just another manifestation of the belief in the existence of irregular time. Most people are waiting for something. A better job, a better car, a better relationship, the list goes on and on.

This, in turn, is simply a way to feed the ego and to create an identity for oneself. Instead of focusing on why you have this belief, it is far better to observe it and then go ahead and do whatever is being indicated to you in the present moment.

Need to Understand the Past

This symptom tends to affect people who are usually academically intelligent, and as a result, they find it tougher to break free than the average person. Since a young age, we've been conditioned to think that the best way to understand something is to get to the bottom of it and to decipher its root cause.

While this is true of academic things, it isn't really the case when it comes to our own emotions. You can delve as deep as you want and try to impose some rationality on your feelings, but you will always fail miserably. People who try doing this usually end up only talking and judging other people's efforts in an attempt to guard themselves against the pain of being reminded that they ought to act, like that other person.

Here's the thing: Let's say you do delve deep into the past and understand why you feel nervous or bitter about certain situations and what triggers your negative emotions. Well, now you've only gone and created an even deeper association with your negative emotions. Rationality is the best way to avert emotional choices.

However, most people seem to think imposing rationality over one's emotions is the way forward. It isn't. Imposing rationality means to simply step into your observer and watch the thinker wring his hands with all sorts of emotions and smile at it. Adopting a non-judgmental attitude is the key to staying in the present. This is what true acceptance is. You are simply observing and being unaffected by those emotions.

The minute you begin to feel those emotions, as in becoming affected by them, you're clinging onto all sorts of lies such as irregular time, your identity, and so on. All of these will be cloaked in various guises, and it is a tiresome exercise to try and decipher the various ways in which the thinker will mislead you.

Instead, refuse to play his game. Take yourself out of the arena entirely by simply watching and smiling. Like a child that realizes that their parent isn't going to return that sweet anytime soon, the thinker will soon figure out that making noise and crying all the time isn't perhaps the best way forward.

The past cannot free you in the present. Instead, it's the other way around. It is the present which frees you from the past and the future and all the shackles that bind you. So, stop analyzing in detail everything that has happened to you and embrace the present moment.

Purpose

When you decide to live in the moment and fully for it, your mind will start throwing curveballs at you with regards to your life's purpose. It will convince you, using your own imperfect understanding of your newfound knowledge, that by simply remaining in the present, watching, and reacting to nature's signals, you're adrift.

As a society, we've been conditioned to be go-getters and to make things happen for ourselves. We value people who refuse to accept their conditions and bend reality to their will, so to speak. From the outside, these people look as if they mold the world around them, but the reality is very different.

The emotional state of a person is the best indicator as to their level of engagement with nature. No matter how wealthy and prosperous one might be, as long as the inner world is not nourished via a healthy connection to nature, it's all for naught. You see, as a society, we've been taught to value just the outer things and ignore the inner.

The reality is that creating the outer manifestation of your desire is most easily done by listening to your inner voice, which is but an extension of natures. Such people are usually marked by a serene calm and equanimity to the world around them. After all, they are doing what nature intended for them to do so why should there ever be a conflict in their world. These people are the true benders of reality.

Ironically, all of this comes about by surrendering to it and not by opposing it. The next time your thinker digs up examples of people who refuse to accept reality and uses them as examples by saying 'look, it worked out for her!', recognize all of this for it really is, just another trap.

By remaining present, you will be able to connect with your inner purpose, and this will manifest in your outer world. You must recognize how perfect this is for you since you do not need to go anywhere but within yourself to understand how to live your best life. People often have the question, "how do I find my purpose?" Well, the answer should be clear by now.

Simply journey within.

An Exercise

Awareness is the key to everything. Once you become aware of and accept things as they are, you will begin to see your life improve by leaps and bounds. Starting from today, keep a note of how you react to problems. Keep a small notebook and a pen or pencil with you at all times and remember to quickly jot down any words that best describe how you feel when you encounter a problem.

If you tend to engage the thinker too much to solve a problem, you'll find that your emotional state will be imbalanced well after finding a solution to the problem, if you ever do find it that is. A mind that is observing most of the time will feel a momentary discomfort, but even that is minimized as a plan to develop a solution is being worked on.

Once a solution I determined, if your mind snaps back to observer mode, you will feel a sense of calm. Track your emotions weekly, and you'll discern a pattern of which emotional triggers take you back into the past. Visualize these triggers occurring to you but with you handling them perfectly and solving the issues and engaging your observer once this is done.

Don't expect miracles, instead, simply enjoy the journey, and recognize how nature has provided you with powerful tools to make your life a dream.

CHAPTER 6

Understanding You

━━━━━━━━━━━━━━━━━━━━━━━━━━━━━

Thus far, we have journeyed into the realms of your mind and seen how it works and affects everything in your life. Through all of this, we have seen how important it is to let go of the illusory "I" that all of us suffer from. This need for identity is not something that is easily let go since almost every one of us has an imperfect relationship with our body.

It is tempting to see the body as a follower of the mind, and in many ways, it is, but that would be simplifying it. You see, your body has almost as much influence on your mind as does your mind on your body. Nothing in creation in senseless, so it follows that the body must have a specific purpose beyond providing a physical form.

In this chapter, we'll see how you can begin to shift your consciousness towards to observer by using your body and by examining why most of us have a poor relationship with it in the first place.

Your Body and You

Every spiritual teaching reduces the body to something like a robot which only listens to the mind's directions. This is a gross misrepresentation of the wonder that the body is, and such representations usually arise from some form of guilt or other negative emotion towards to body.

The body's regular functions are where we observe ourselves at our most animal-like form. Just like animals, we have the need to feed it, protect it, clean it, treat it when it experiences disease, and use it to procreate. This last quality has been the most problematic of all, for religion and spirituality in general.

With most religions and societies, man is taken to be the highest form of creation as granted. How then, does one reconcile the fact that man occupies the exact same shell and experiences the exact same needs as these so-called lower life forms? The need to procreate is the most basic function every species has, but it is only man who questions it and is fearful of it.

This fear has led to many societies demonizing sexuality as the work of the devil and as something to be guarded against, at all costs, lest it corrupt society and destroy it. All of this is once again, the thinker doing what he does best. In requiring an identity that is distinct and above those of other life forms, man deploys his thinker to find any and every reason to deny his most basic nature.

This only leads to a loss of connection with it and results in enormous guilt and repression. Many societies go the other way and in the name of embracing nature, end up practicing hedonism and lose all sense of proportion and balance. This need not apply to just sexuality, but to anything we hinge our identity upon.

The greater the list of things you use to define yourself as "you," the greater you disconnect with nature and reality. It should come as no surprise that societies which experience the greatest of imbalances, be it repressive or overly expressive, are either the most violent or the most economically backward and insular on this planet.

Understanding and getting in touch with the true nature of your body is the key out of this mess.

The Inner You

Let us take a step back and review some things we have learned. We know that nature has created everything from largely the same material, no matter how distinct it may look to our unevolved eyes. If our body happens to share the same instincts and needs as that of animals, it stands to reason then that nature resides within our body.

When we speak of the connection between our minds and nature, what we're really talking about is our minds finding the source of nature within ourselves. This is why a journey inward is the most enlightening since the nature of everything can be discovered within. Our body is made of the same substance as everything else is.

Journeying within, by engaging our observer, also free up our mental faculty, resources that the thinker usually uses to serve the ego, to deeply understand and perceive the entire universe within us. The body, you see is the receptacle within which nature resides within us. It flows with life, which is but an expression of nature and its blessing upon us.

Your body has an inner energy which ebbs and flows depending on your thoughts and physical situation. How many times have you felt fear physically before becoming aware of it? The body has a language of its own and is in constant contact with the observer within you. You only need to tune into the frequency.

Your journey inward will provide you with very valuable insight. As you realize how much in common you have with nature, that indeed, you are nature itself manifested in physical form, your illusion of being separate of having a distinct "I" will dissolve. Only then will you realize the trivial nature of most of your questions and doubts.

Distance always brings perspective. We're too caught up within our own perceived reality and the everyday mundanities of our existence that we have forgotten what it is like to take a step back and simply observe our role in the bigger picture. Journeying within puts you in touch with greater realities, a reality far more complex in design and purpose, that you cannot help but be quiet and admire its magnificence.

The Buddha taught that humanity's core error was to assume that we are nothing more than some combination of our body and mind. This great illusion is one of the biggest reasons for suffering. It is only by realizing this error that we can be free from the greatest sin of them all: The sin of harming ourselves.

Transformation

The unnatural way to approach your transformation would be to attempt it via the religiously recommended route. This usually involves some form of deprivation, either of food, water, or sex, and is rooted in the incorrect belief that the body's natural instincts need to be curbed. That evolution means rising above as opposed to greater assimilation with the greater force.

Meditation is one form of journey within and is hugely beneficial in all forms. Whether it is observing your breath or simply observing the life force within you, meditation will force your observer into action, and this is the correct way to transform your life and mind through your body.

Always reserve a portion of your attention on your inner life force. What this means is, whenever you're performing a task, always ensure the observer is engaged in recognizing the sensations and life-defining forces that are coursing within you. An example of this is your heartbeat or your breath, and these are the more obvious signs.

As you become more and more accustomed to observing yourself, you'll realize that life is nothing but pure energy and that this energy is enormous and is in constant connection with everything around you. Recall, have you ever felt someone before noticing they're nearby? Have you ever looked at the door and just felt that someone is behind it?

These are all examples of how the life energy within us communicates with the greater energy around us and how each and every life form carries a small part of it within itself. When journeying within, always listen to your boy and do not fight it. Do not go against its wishes and try to impose your own order over it. You might as well try to impose your order over the whole world in that instant.

Your body is your gateway to nature and to a force infinitely cleverer than you. Simply go with the tide and follow the directions.

Your Body and the Now

Having deep-rooted connections to your body at all times is the best way to remain present and to stay out of the untrained thinker's clutches. You see, the thinker is very much like a child, except one with great power. The more attention you give him, the more spoiled he becomes.

The solution to getting the thinker working for you is to starve him of attention. When this is done, whenever you do decide to get back to him, the thinker will be more than eager to oblige your every wish. Thus, stay in the now, the present moment, and stay in touch with nature in order to transform everything in your life.

Perform attention checks as much as possible. Right now, ask yourself where your attention is. Is it on this book entirely? Are you aware of physical sensations within you? Are you aware of the heat and cold within you? Any pain or stress? Is your mind focused on something else? Regularly checking in is much like a ping on a submarine's sonar. It serves the dual purpose of mapping out the way forward and getting a good picture of its own surroundings.

From the journal you've created as an exercise in the previous chapter, recognize what your inner state felt like when you went through any challenge. How do you feel now if you face a challenge? The key to severing the connection between the emotional thinker and the challenge is to quickly journey within the moment you encounter a challenge.

This way, you're forcing your observer to get in charge and are dissociating the moment from your thinker. Observing the energy within your even for a split second has enormous benefits for you to deploy your thinker creatively, that is to find solutions, instead of running around from the past to the future.

If you're worried about not reacting to a challenge or worried that the challenge will overcome you if you don't react, remember, you're getting in touch with nature by doing this. Nature wants you to succeed, and nothing will make it happier. Stands to reason then that getting in touch with nature is the thing to do when faced with a tough situation.

The Aging Process

Your inner environment is a very different place from your outer body. Both the inner and the outer experience of aging. While there isn't anything one can do about the outer body aging, the inner body is an entirely different matter. When thinking of the inner body, we ought to look at it as a mix between our spirit and nature.

This combination is nothing but the energy that courses within us. Someone who is always present in their body, via their attention and focus, will be able to get rid of any parasitic emotions that grip them from time to time. By merely being present, we can shine the light of awareness on the issue and root it out. Recall what we learned earlier about removing darkness. The thing to do is to simply shine the light on it.

This explains why despite looking old, some people don't feel old, both to themselves and to others around them. Have you ever wondered why some people age gracefully and others don't? While genetics and taking care of your outer body does play a role, this pales in significance to the difference that having a buoyant inner body makes. If you're full of life within, you will be full of life without.

As you journey within, you will also realize another truth. The inner body is not bound by time. It is spirit and energy, and this cannot grow old by any means. While it may become jaded, energy is always transformed into another form; it can never be destroyed. The more you begin to identify with your inner form, the more you will come to realize that time is a man-made construct. The reality is that there is no time, only awareness and the now.

Your presence within will also help you rectify any damaging emotions and thoughts that take residence within your mind. This is simply because every emotion that the mind undergoes, the body has to express. Think about it, can you tell just by looking at someone that they are happy? Sad? Excited? The body always conveys what the mind is undergoing, no matter how much of a poker face one might possess.

By staying at home, so to speak, you will be able to ensure on desired house guests take up residence, and those who cause problems are more than welcome to stay out. Thus, your psychological well-being will improve, and as a result, have a rejuvenating effect on your body, which will refresh your mind and so on.

The Importance of Surrender

While it's all well and good to read the words in this book and think to yourself that this is great and everything, you will need to go ahead and practice everything as a part of your daily life. A major obstacle that most people put in front of themselves is with regards to their attitude.

Practice is a lot more than just following the steps mentioned in the exercises listed thus far in this book. You will need to begin with your mind first. A lot of people merely practice with their bodies but ignore the mind. Then they act surprised when the body doesn't comply. It never will because your mind is not in the correct state.

Everything begins with surrender. This is a tough word for those of us who have grown up in traditional Western society. The act of surrender implies defeat, and there's nothing worse than this. If this word disturbs you, think of it as going with the flow or taking the path of least resistance. Anytime you practice the techniques taught in this book, tell yourself you are simply going with the flow.

By doing this, you're preparing your mind for what is to come and reassuring your thinker that he can settle down and thus, engage the observer better. Once you begin to experience the positive effects of being present, your mind will surrender all on its own. The practice described below demands surrender, or else you're unlikely to derive any benefit from it.

Before going to bed, as you first lie down, take a few deep breaths, and relax into your body. Feel how loose every part of you is and if there is any tension you feel, relax it consciously by taking a few deep breaths and noticing how the tension dissipates. Next, begin your journey inward by scanning your body from head to toe for any signs of life.

What this means is any sensation, any force or feeling that you can detect, go ahead and observe it. Remember, pain is a sensation as is sound. So, if you can hear anything in your environment, notice it for a short time, without any judgment and then resume your bodily scan. Keep the scans up for as long as you can, and eventually, you'll find yourself drifting off into a restful sleep.

The first few times you do this, you'll likely feel sensations on just your outer physical body. After a while, though, you will begin to feel a force inward. While there's no accurate way of describing this inner force, you will feel your outer body melt away and merely be conscious of the life energy within you. This energy is full of vitality and you will realize how nourishing it is.

Self-discipline

CHAPTER 7

Understanding Presence

Being present sounds like an easy enough thing to do. After all, it's just about noticing what's going on in the moment, right? Well, theoretically yes, but practically, it's a lot more complicated than that. People often have an idea of what presence is, intellectually, but fail to practice it. You can never understand the presence by merely thinking about it or forming an idea about it.

You need to go ahead and practice. The reason is this: Your thinker doesn't understand what presence is, given its time-bound nature. The Observer doesn't bother with understanding anything, merely observing. Hence, thinking about presence is a bit of an oxymoron. You need to go ahead and feel it via practice.

Enhancing the Presence

Presence can be best defined as recognizing the oneness of everything, starting with you. We tend to think of our body and mind as being two halves of ourselves, but the reality is that they are two and one. Fully communicative with one another and unable to survive without the other, yet distinct in character.

The best way to experience a dose of presence is by doing the following practice: Close your eyes right now and ask yourself "What is going to come next within my head?" and simply be alert for the next thought that enters. Be watchful. What do you experience?

Deep Roots

We saw in the last chapter how necessary it is to have deep roots within oneself. The previous exercise is an example of how you can establish these roots and how you can quiet your mind. You are living in your body fully and completely, and chances are that you had to wait for a longer than usual period for a thought to enter.

You can't go about your daily life doing this, of course. The best thing to do is to simply not expect the same level of emptiness in your mind, as you experienced in the exercise, as you go about your day. This would be unrealistic. Instead, adopt an attitude of waiting and stillness.

This waiting is very different from the waiting that was described as a mistake previously. The former waiting is bound to time and is anticipating something in the future to heal the present. That attitude engages the thinker fully and increases your ego's dependence on emotion.

This attitude of waiting is more about waiting to see what happens next, much like in the exercise. It conveys an understanding that the present moment is all that matters and that you are ever alert, ready to interpret and act on whatever nature communicates to you. There is no time or judgment. There is no emotion since you don't know what will happen.

There is only the stillness of anticipation and alertness. When you are in such a state, you will observe your mind going blank. In the initial stages, these gaps will last for just a few seconds, and you'll be astonished at how refreshing they will be. Once you experience it, you will want more simply because this is a reflection of your true nature.

The Creative Mechanism

We've covered the nature of your inbuilt creative mechanism previously. The thing about your creative instinct is that it can only act in the present, now moment. Being an extension of nature, there is no past or future it recognizes. It can only detect the issue or problem on hand and react to it.

The key to solving your problems then is to simply relax and trust it to work. Unfortunately, most of us are conditioned to 'think' our way out of trouble by using our so-called rational thinking power. While rationality is the correct choice, we're deluding ourselves by expecting our thinker to provide rational thought.

Rational thought, or the correct choice, only comes from nature. To receive this, we need to listen. Hence, the advice to relax and surrender to nature and simply trust your creative instinct to take over and come up with solutions for you. Most of us cloud this with thoughts and anxiety about the results and outcomes of our actions.

Doing this only blocks your connection and ironically, results in poor outcomes. Free yourself from worrying about results and using the thinker to preoccupy yourself about the outcomes of your actions. Again, this is not to say that worry and anxiety are invalid emotions.

Merely that, they should be confined to the initial stages of your thought when you're forming your plans. At this stage, these negative emotions play a vital role in forming what is called 'defensive pessimism,' which cautions you to check and double check everything. However, once plans have been laid out, they serve no further purpose since there's nothing you can do about it now. So let them go and relax into consciousness.

Perception and Thought

The key characteristic of the observer is that it has no voice. After all, why would it need one? The observer helps you slow down and understand perception and thought are two very different things. It will help you understand where and how thought originates. Thought is merely a representation of a mental image that has been stored previously in your head.

When you observe something as part of your daily life, the processes of perception and thought are so rushed that they seem to be a single process. You look at something, and immediately, a thought rushes into your head. However, whenever you go into nature and look at some natural phenomena, perhaps a huge mountain, a deep valley, the endless desert, or the vast, impersonal nature of the ocean, you generally relapse into silence.

Why is this? It's because your thinker simply doesn't have any mental imagery to provide you with thought. All you can do is be present since the thinker, for once is forced to shut up and be quiet. The observer steps into the void, and all you do is observe and feel the life force within you. This is what being present feels like. If you've ever felt this, then you'll understand how such a feeling cannot be described fully by words.

The time it takes for you to perceive something and react with thought is an indicator of your presence. You might think this would be easier if all the pictures you were faced with were awe-inspiring, instead of the daily mundane things you encounter. However, take a closer look around you. Don't you see the miracle that this world is? We take so many things for granted and even abuse nature, but can you see how nature still cares very deeply about us and continues to provide means to further ourselves?

To one who is present, there is a miracle even in something as ordinary as a potholed road. You should not strive to become someone like this since this is just focusing on the end goal. Instead, you should simply relax and surrender to the moment. Go where it takes you and trust that your creative instinct will solve whatever comes your way.

Creative Flashes

Have you ever heard stories of people who were taking a nap and then suddenly jumped up and down, realizing they found a solution to a problem they were facing? There's the famous story of Archimedes who ran naked through the streets of ancient Athens screaming "Eureka," thanks to receiving a flash of knowledge when taking a bath.

Why does it always seem as if flashes of creativity occur when we perform mundane, everyday tasks? The answer is because when doing the mundane, we tend to switch off our thinker and only engage the observer. In this relaxed state, we are fully connected to nature, and nature provides us with all the solutions we need.

Another common experience is receiving flashes of intuition or solutions while half asleep. We oscillate between deep sleep and half consciousness when we go to sleep, and the state of deep sleep is when our connection with nature is at its strongest. Unfortunately for us, our conscious brain is off and only when we become half-conscious do we realize the mental picture that has been planted there by nature, to aid us.

If all of this sounds unbelievable to you, here's a story about the Swiss geologist Louis Agassiz, as told by his wife, recorded in the book Psycho-Cybernetics by Dr. Maxwell Maltz (Maltz and Powers, 2010) 1:

"He had been striving to decipher the somewhat obscure impression of a fossil fish on the stone slab in which it was preserved. Weary and perplexed, he put his work aside at last and tried to dismiss it from his mind. Shortly after, he waked one night persuaded that while asleep, he had seen his fish with all the missing features perfectly restored.

He went early to the Jardin des Plantes, thinking that on looking anew at the impression he would see something to put him on the track of his vision. In vain — the blurred record was as blank as ever. The next night he saw the fish again, but when he waked, it disappeared from his memory as before. Hoping the same experience might be repeated, on the third night, he placed a pencil and paper beside his bed before going to sleep.

Towards morning the fish reappeared in his dream, confusedly at first, but at last with such distinctness that he no longer had any doubt as to its zoological characters. Still half dreaming, in perfect darkness, he traced these characters on the sheet of paper at the bedside. In the morning he was surprised to see in his nocturnal sketch features which he thought it impossible the fossil itself would reveal. He hastened to the Jardin des Plantes and, with his drawing as a guide, succeeded in chiselling away the surface of the stone under which portions of the fish proved to be hidden. When wholly exposed, the fossil corresponded with his dream and his drawing, and he succeeded in classifying it with ease."

Physical Elements of Presence

While presence is an intense mental activity, your body and physical form will do a lot to contribute to your feeling of presence. Much like how slouching when reading will cause you to feel sleepy and miss the words you're trying to grasp, every physical posture you adopt has an equivalent mental state that will be produced.

In this section, we will go through some aspects of your physical being, which will help enhance your connection to the present.

Posture

According to Zen Buddhist teachings, your posture is your practice, in and as of itself. That is, correct posture is enlightenment by itself. While a traditional zen monk will spend most of their day in meditation, this is not of much practical use to you. However, your aim when going about your day should be to adopt a posture that is best suited for the task at hand, in order to enhance your alertness.

Driving is a common task everyone performs. Would it make sense for you to lean your seat all the way back and grasp the steering wheel with just your fingertips? No, this would almost certainly result in an accident. You see, practicing presence isn't about sitting in a meditation cell cross-legged and chanting something.

It is being fully aware of everything you're currently doing. When eating food, how much attention are you really paying to the flavor, the taste, the texture, and so on of the thing you're eating? Most of us tend to watch television while eating. Posture implies both physical and mental awareness. If you think eating your food is boring and that you need some other activity to keep you entertained while you do it, you're probably not looking hard enough.

Breath

Some people make the mistake, thanks to an imperfect understanding of meditation, of trying to equate presence with breathing. By this logic, controlling your breath is the way forward. This is an immature understanding of what presence means. You should never have any expectation of outcomes to begin with, including what your breath ought to be like.

Instead of worrying about the fact that your breath is not soft and shallow, simply observe it without judgment. Your breath is an excellent way for you to become rooted to your body since it is an automatic mechanism that you do not need to prompt. It will go on and on until the day it stops.

Observe how your breath changes as your external situations change. This will help you develop a better idea of how rooted you are and how your degree of presence changes depending on your external motivations.

Your Need to Control

We've been conditioned from a very young age that we need to control things around us and that we can influence everything. If we follow the logic of the creative instinct and of how nature provides us with solutions we need, this is true. We can create the things we desire.

However, the approach to this sort of creation is counterintuitive. Our first instinct is to think that to create something we need to be deeply involved in every step of its creation and that we should dictate each and every step that is taken to help realize it. Needless to say, this works when we create a physical object, but when it comes to a life form created by nature, it almost always results in disaster.

Much like caging a bird, you cannot control things that occur in nature, and this includes your mind. You cannot command it to stop thinking of things other than your breath. It will do what it wants to do. Your job is to rise above it and to observe, preferably with a smile, its nature and how it constantly tries to torment itself.

We've used an example of a child to describe the mind previously, and the analogy fits here as well. If you have a child, trying to control them by dictating each and every minute of their day will only lead to them to rebel and probably hate your every fiber. The best way to guide or instruct them is to provide them with a framework of rules and then sit back and watch as they do whatever it is they do. One can see the same phenomenon when visiting a farm.

Place an animal within a small enclosure, and it usually gets agitated. Place it on a bigger field though, it doesn't notice the boundary fence and is quite content to stay in place. Your discipline and practice function, much like the boundary fence for your thoughts. Your task is to observe and let them roam wherever they want, fully knowing that they won't come to real harm as long as they're within the fence.

Once they breach the fence, you step in and take action to correct their course. The trick, of course, is to realize where the boundaries lie, and this is where observation comes into play. Trial and error during your practice will give you the best idea as to where you need to place your fence.

The first step though, is to realize that you control things by giving up control. You win by surrendering. You become free through discipline. Understand these seemingly dichotomous principles, and you'll enhance your understanding of the world by leaps and bounds.

Practice

While your practice should be continuous, you should set aside time during your day to simply sit and observe yourself. Close your eyes, relax by taking a few deep breaths, and adopt a posture that will enable you to stay alert and not fall asleep.

Begin by observing your breath as detailed in a previous exercise. Observe which nostril air is exiting and entering from and the nature of this breath. Gently move from observing your breath to observing the top of your head for any sensations that might be occurring there. Remember to not change anything or to modify anything that is happening, simply observe.

Next work your way down from your head, down your scalp and your ears to your chest. Notice everything that you can about your chest, the sensations you feel, whether you can feel your heart beating or not. Remember to no go looking for specific sensations, simply observe what is already going on. If you can't feel anything, just observe and be aware of how your clothes feel against your skin.

Moving down from chest, via your stomach, move down your legs, again simply observing what is going on and not changing a thing. Remember that pain is a sensation, as in numbness, and keep observing. Move back up your body via the back of your legs and your back, repeating the process the whole time.

When focusing on a particular body part, you will feel a sensation elsewhere. For example, when focusing on your head, your legs might hurt. Your mind will be distracted for an instant but strive to keep bringing it back to the relevant place in your body as much as possible.

The idea here is not to control your mind but to train it to narrow its focus gently. Do not expect any miracles when performing this and simply recognize that the practice, in and as of itself, is what counts the most.

CHAPTER 8

Understanding Relationships

Your relationships contain a ton of information about where you are in your life. People seem to know this innately and often to cover past wounds; they seek new relationships to make them whole again. Relationships, as covered in this chapter, include both romantic as well as platonic.

The most relationship of all is, of course, the one you have with yourself. Given the advice this book has provided thus far about letting go of the need for an "I," it might seem strange advocating such a relationship. However, there is a place for it.

Truly loving relationships offer a path to enlightenment, or salvation if you prefer that word, because a relationship brings together a lot of things that enable us to move closer to nature. As human beings, we are naturally half of a whole. That is, our polarity is either masculine or feminine. This is not a reference to our sex but to our inner polarity.

Every person has a mixture of both but tends to lean to one side favorably. So, it is possible to have a man (sex) who has a feminine polarity and a woman (sex) who has a masculine polarity. Romantic relationships tend to order themselves as a union between masculine and feminine, based on the polarity, and it is with this that we shall concern ourselves.

Our outer sex may or may not be an accurate representation of our inner polarity, which is closer to nature and is what should be listened to.

Love and Romance

Human beings search for relationships as an effort to approach becoming whole. All of us are essentially halves of humanity, and a relationship with the opposite polarity gives us a chance at becoming whole. Sexual intercourse provides a physical method by which we can become whole, but even this moment is fleeting and does not last long.

A lot of relationships are based on an unhealthy love/hate stereotype, which is just the ego's way of trying to assert an identity. Most times, this search for identity even dictates who we wish to be with, going as far as to ignore people with whom we share a true connection and instead of chasing after some ideal according to the ego's definition of it.

All of this lays the basis for relationships to become toxic after a while.

Love to Love/Hate

This is the usual pattern that plays out when it comes to relationships. During the initial phases, both parties are deeply in love with one another and are infatuated. Neither of them can do any wrong. This sort of love is fleeting simply because the intensity of it cannot be maintained over a long time.

A lot of couples make the mistake of mistaking this infatuation for true love, and once the high disappears, they think their love has faded. All they're left with now is this imperfect person who doesn't have a halo around them anymore. The frustration of losing the 'loving' feeling leads to people blaming their partners, and soon, the fault finding starts.

In an effort to justify the loss of 'love,' every single fault is nit-picked, and the bickering becomes constant. The real tragedy is that people think this is normal and that once the honeymoon period is over, one needs to simply tolerate the partner one is with. In short, that initial love that united the couple has now become the reason for them to resent one another.

This kind of backward reasoning is possible only when you act from the ego's perspective. The ego is constantly searching for drama to feed itself, and there's no more fertile ground than a relationship. The very act of mental and physical union with a partner opens you up like nothing else because suddenly, you begin to live outside of yourself, and for someone else.

This union is detrimental to the strength of the ego since a union means the loss of personal identity. Given this fact, the ego then tries to trick you in two ways. One, it tried to convince you to build an identity based on the relationship as a whole. Examples of this are when you begin to lose sight of yourself as an individual in a relationship or when you label the two of you with an image ('the power couple,' 'the artistic couple' etc.).

Just to clarify, seeing yourself as an individual in a relationship doesn't mean looking at your identity as being subjugated by the union. You are one part of nature uniting with another. Both of you, representing different parts of the whole are equally important, and there is no dominant and subordinate in this. If you lose sight of you being a part of nature and as only deriving meaning from the union, you're effectively ending the union since you're giving yourself up.

Meanwhile, once the ego has tricked you into deriving an identity for yourself, your relationship becomes a vehicle for it, and this is how your vessel of love becomes a vessel of love/hate. The drama that this dynamic generates becomes heaven for the ego, and therefore one often witnesses couples staying together in a drama filled relationships.

Addiction

Even if a person does decide to break out of this poisonous relationship, you'll often see them desperately searching for someone new to get attached to. Often, the ego will convince them to choose a partner who is completely wrong for them. Once that relationship goes bad, the person often wonders what they were thinking of in the first place.

Well, this need for being in a relationship is the ego's need to validate its identity and to feed itself. It is nothing short of an addiction. People consume all sorts of intoxicants, in excess, to cover up emotional scars. They lack the courage to face up to it due to the perceived pain they think they will have to go through. A lot of people turn to romantic relationships to soothe themselves over their perceived inadequacy.

The fact that they have a partner gives them validation and helps them cover up their scars and run away from their problems. This is exactly why pursuing a relationship to make you whole or believing that a relationship will cure all your problems is incorrect thinking.

Healthy Relationships

The first step to recovery is to understand that your lack of presence is a major cause for bad relationships. A lack of presence means a lack of awareness about your emotional scars which you need to heal, whether a relationship exists or not.

Following on from everything we've learned thus far, it should be obvious from the previous section how most relationships becomes vessels for identity and show a strong belief in the validity of irregular time. Thinking you will be whole once you're in a relationship is no different from thinking you'll be richer once you get that new job.

The thinker gets hyperactive when it comes to evaluating a relationship, even before it has started, and it can be quite difficult to determine who exactly is being engaged. A key sign is to examine yourself and evaluate whether any hate is present as a part of your love. Hate could be anything from obsessiveness, possessiveness, jealousy, insecurity, and so on.

Only in the emotional world of the thinker does love contain hate. In nature's world, the real world, true love has no hate or anything else attached to it. It is denoted by acceptance, complete, and unconditional. When your partner fails to meet your expectation, examine yourself for your reactions. Do you react from an egocentric position, taking the shortfall as a slight to yourself, or do you react in a selfless manner?

All our partners will fall short of our expectations. This is normal. True love is finding perfection in imperfection and understanding what that means. Much like finding stillness, this is a feeling that is experienced and cannot be fully described. The way to finding it is to journey inward and simply observe. Nature will light the way for you, and you will find true love.

Love, of course, comes in many forms. While the major focus this far has been romantic relationships, everything discussed applies equally to friendship, family, and so on. One of the keys to enlightened relationships is to recognize the piece of nature that is within you, underneath your flaws and your mistake as well as recognize them in your partner.

Just as you are a part of nature, so is your partner. Accept this and move forward. The minute true acceptance is achieved, both of you will move beyond your egos and into the present moment. Once you're accustomed to being present with yourself, you will eventually begin to feel the life that courses within you, the piece of nature within.

Once you recognize this, you will soon recognize this in your partner as well, and then your relationship will seem as if it has been ordained by nature as if some greater power brought the two of you together. Your feelings for your partner move well beyond the physical form and beyond mere egos. This is where true love resides.

For true love to flourish, you need to move beyond the mere physical and become rooted in the present.

Practice

Relationships increase the intensity with which your thinker gets activated. On the one hand, this can be a problem. The tidal wave of emotion and neurotic thinking that will be thrown your way is a major challenge. However, with every challenge comes opportunity.

A lot of problems occur in the first place because of the unrealistic expectations of an ideal relationship or partner. Acceptance of the fact that there is no such thing is a great place to start. This is indeed the truth about nature as well. As individuals, none of us is perfect, but the whole we add up to makes nature and this world perfect.

As you recognize this truth and practice it with all your relationships, you will come closer to having healthy relationships and forming real bonds with the loved ones in your life. Above all else, you must realize that no one can transform or change another person. To do this is to assume that you know better than nature, which is just another way of assuming an identity for your ego to feed on.

Acceptance involves identifying and observing all the imperfections that exist. Much like how you journeyed inward to establish roots within yourself, you will have to journey into the nature of your relationship and become aware of all its imperfections. Once you realize what they way, accept them. If there's jealousy, accept it. If there's anger, accept it.

The reflex action in such instances is to try to further break down what causes these feelings to occur and to try and make them go away. However, remember that the best way of banishing darkness is to simply shine a light on it. By becoming aware of and remaining with the jealousy and observing it, without identifying with it or judging it, you will see it diminish and eventually disappear.

You and Your Partner

This attitude of nonjudgment is something you will need to extend to your partner as well. A lot of people get frustrated when their partner doesn't follow through on steps they themselves have taken. Remember, you are an individual in a relationship, a part of a whole. You are not responsible for your partner's actions any more than you are for your neighbors.

A lot of people tend to see defects in their partner and want to change them. This is not a method to change your partner, and you should not attempt to do so. Acceptance of who they are is the first step. There is no outcome here other than a loving relationship, and the journey itself is enlightenment, not the outcome.

Whenever you observe your partner behaving in an inadequate or imperfect manner, simply observe and do not judge. You may react from a natural standpoint, at the moment, but take care to not attach labels to their actions. By remaining with the light of nature and acting from this standpoint, your partner cannot help but observe the loving space you are providing them with.

As a result, they will seek to rise in awareness themselves and will take your cues. Again, remember, the journey is the point. This is not supposed to be done with the aim of changing your partner somehow. If you try to do so, you're imposing judgment on them and this, removing yourself from the now moment.

People who are meant to remain together are usually reflections of another, from nature's point of view. If you improve your actions and remain present, your partner will soon follow you. If they do not, the two of you will find ways to become separate. As such, there is no need for you to worry about your relationship or whether your partner is right for you.

All you must do is to be present and observe as nature directs you along a course to your greatest benefit.

You and the Collective

As people, all of us tend to think of ourselves are belonging to certain groups. Even if you have absolutely no religious, national, or ethnic identity that you feel a part of, your sex will provide some form of identity within you. This is especially true of women, who tend to view each other as belonging to a greater sisterhood.

The reasons for this is not relevant, beyond noting that the largely patriarchal nature of most societies tends to help women bond closer over shared pain. Whatever the reasons might be, your identity, to the extent that you identify with the collective, will be a source of pain for you.

Pain that emanates thanks to the problems and oppression faced by your sex is hard to let go of. After all, our sex is constantly present with us, physically and emotionally. We cannot simply let it dissolve, and achieving this is something that takes more than a lifetime of doing.

Please note that renouncing one identity to claim another is not giving anything up. For example, renouncing yourself as a woman and identifying as nonbinary is not renouncing anything but merely switching identities. As such, letting go of your need to identify with particular sex is part of your struggle to sever the "I" in your life.

The key is to start with the correct expectations; in other words, have none. Whenever pain arises, or conflict arises, from whichever source, simply stay present with it and observe it. Observe the changes it tries to make to you, how it tries to manifest within you and stay with it. You'll soon see the emotion subsides and nature providing a path for you to move forward.

You

Where does your relationship with yourself fit into all of this, you might be wondering? An alternative question might be if one is fully present and conscious of nature, is it even necessary to be in a relationship?

Well, given that your physical form is not whole, a relationship is something which is necessary in your life. It is very rare for a person to achieve full and total awareness of nature by their lonesome. As for the relationship with oneself, perhaps a better way to think of this is to simply be.

Instead of seeking to define and worry about self-love or hate, why not just be with yourself? Accept and observe, observe and accept, without judgment or any reaction whatsoever, and you will see the parts of nature within you make themselves evident.

This will naturally lead to greater, unconditional love within you since this is the true essence of nature. You see, letting go of your identity or your need for an "I" is simply getting closer to nature and dissolving within it.

This doesn't mean you need to deprive yourself of anything because nature is not some cruel mistress who demands such sacrifices. All you need to do is to be aware, and nature will come forward and reveal itself. You cannot but follow its path once this happens.

CHAPTER 9

Understanding Peace

eople often cannot distinguish the difference between happiness and peace and thus, end up confusing the two of them. So how is happiness distinguished from peace? Simply put, happiness is the state of being that is dependent on the external, on an illusory form. It is transient and non-permanent.

Peace, on the other hand, is harder to attain but is more permanent in nature. Peace implies acceptance and acceptance can only arise by living in the present and seeing things for what they are. There are a lot of important concepts contained within this so let's unpack all of them one by one.

Drama

When we're living through our egos, we perceive the world through binary results. Good/bad, rich/poor, happy/unhappy, and so on. We rush towards the perceived good or happy experiences and seek to avoid the bad ones. From a logical standpoint, this makes sense: After all, the more desirable experiences one has in their life, the happier they will be?

This is far from the case, though. There are just as many depressed billionaires as there is regular folk. Just as many obstacles in their lives as there are in other people's. Clearly, happiness cannot be bought. So, what's the solution then?

The Way to Peace

Acceptance and allowance of the present moment is the key to inner peace. As explained before, happiness is an outer mechanism, completely dependent on something you cannot control. There is no way for you to control the events in your life since this depends on the actions of millions of other people and events far beyond your control. Thus, allowing the present moment to pass through you is the way forward.

This doesn't mean you need to be idle and sit back doing nothing. A lot of people think of acceptance as a passive state, but the reality is very different. When you've accepted the present state for what it is, your mind is free from the ego's need for emotional drama, and you will see that every event had a kernel of wisdom in it, no matter how bad it might seem on the surface.

If a loved one dies, does this mean you should not be unhappy? No. This is misunderstanding what acceptance is. Understand that happiness and sadness are external creations and are impermanent. All that can be permanent is within you. It is perfectly possible to be unhappy and yet, at peace. You will mourn the loss of a loved one, but this does not mean your inner core needs to be shaken.

Every negative event or trauma contains wisdom within it; some lesson the universe feels we need to learn to move forward. Remember, the universe is a benevolent being and not a vindictive one. Much like a parent who needs to discipline a child that is eating far too many sweets, the universe needs to apply negative pressure to us in order for us to see the light.

The more you ignore its signs, by living in the past or future, the greater the negative trauma it will need to apply to get you to snap back to the present moment. Using the child and parent example, a child that repeatedly disobeys its parent will undergo a harsher punishment than one that does listen and understands the parent's intention behind their actions.

Therefore, some people suffer repeated negative experiences, each one worse than the last. Acceptance of the present will help you deal with the negativity since you will be freed from your ego and be able to see the way forward. It is in this way forward that your lesson lies and eventually, enlightenment.

Let go of your need for happiness and your dependence on anything external. It is only by doing this that you will be able to let go of the drama that plagues your life, which is but an expression of your ego.

Impermanence

What is the one thing all external things have in common? They're impermanent. Everything you see around you, including your physical form is impermanent. The only permanent thing about you is your core energy, and at our lower level of consciousness, we simply don't know what happens to this once our physical form declines.

This is another way of saying we don't know what happens after we die. Our physical form is reduced to dust. No matter who you are or how amazing your life currently is or how bad and unbearable it is, within a period of 70 years from now, your form will be dust.

Viewed in this light, what does it matter how good or bad your external factors are? Sure, take pleasure in your happiness when it occurs, feel sad when something goes against you, but remember, there is no peace in becoming attached to a particular event or thing. Allow everything to pass through you, as if you are transparent.

On a higher plane of consciousness, there is no good or bad since everything that happens points a way forward for you. It is up to you to decipher the signs and be aware of what the present moment is communicating to you.

Thus, no matter whether your life is on the up and up or whether you're going through a prolonged period of misfortune, everything has wisdom for you to learn within it. If you feel sad thanks to external factors, such as all your peers moving ahead of you in life, remember, all of that is illusory and impermanent.

It is like saying you'll be happy only because it is spring. Well, spring doesn't last forever. It changes to summer which morphs to fall and winter. Without knowing the depths of cold during winter, you cannot enjoy the beautiful sunshine in spring. Without feeling the searing heat of summer, you cannot appreciate the beauty of a chilly fall morning.

Notice the wisdom of everything and observe how it is only human beings who experience feelings of euphoria and depression. Such feelings are caused by a lack of wisdom with regards to impermanence. Overt attachment to feelings of happiness causes both euphoria and depression, as does overt attachment to sadness.

Who among us had ever witnessed a depressed bird? A sad bird, yes. But a depressed one? How many of you have seen shows on TV which depicts a lion hunting on the plains of Africa? Have you ever noticed how the deer reacts to an unsuccessful hunt, in other words, once it escapes the literal jaws of death?

It goes back to eating grass. It doesn't sit around worrying about what it did wrong or even pat itself on the back for what it did right. It doesn't worry about where the next attack will come from. Once it ascertains there are no predators about, it goes back to eating grass.

The deer doesn't have the ability to create what it wants as humans do. Unfortunately, none of us know how to wield our creative mechanism and end up creating hell for ourselves. Depression and euphoria are simply symptoms of all this.

A lesson that derives from all of this is the fact that nothing matters much. This does cause some sense of sadness upon the first realization, and it is normal to experience this. This sadness is simply you finally letting go of your ego. You've lived with something for so long and have grown so attached to it; it is natural to feel a sense of bereavement.

Your ego, in a last-ditch effort, will try to trick you into thinking that since nothing matters, you need not strive to do anything or achieve anything. Nothing matters, right? Well, if you follow this path, you will never achieve peace. Inner peace is the degree to which all of us have evolved in our lives and have learned our lessons from the collection of present moments throughout our lives.

Thus, if you do not have peace, you are not in acceptance of the present. Therefore, the ego, as usual, is wrong. Understanding lies in acceptance. Accept that yes, perhaps nothing matters and that you don't know what that means. The act of doing so will reveal nature's wisdom to you.

Compassion

The Dalai Lama once said, 'If you wish to be truly selfish, be compassionate.' There is a lot of wisdom in that quote, which will take a lot more than just this book to unpack. What is compassion? As a minimal definition, it is the ability to empathize with another's condition.

The degree of compassion is a true marker of peace within someone. When you have let go of yourself, of time, of your ego and your need to be 'happy' all the time, what else is left? Your surroundings. Once you open your eyes to them, you will notice the wisdom with which nature operates and realize that what exists in you exists in everything else.

In the end, all is one.

Reality

We've broached the subject of reality many times throughout this book. Here it bears to note that reality exists on a single plane when viewed through the ego. There is your reality, and that is it. The ego forces your reality on everything else and makes you think that your reality is the only one within the universe.

This is a bit like saying there's only one truth throughout the universe, a patently absurd statement! As you journey through your path and find greater levels of inner peace, you will realize that your reality is an illusion and is impermanent, much like everything else to do with 'you.'

Simultaneously, you will realize that the universal reality is an amalgam of millions and billions of realities spread throughout the universe that serve to make up its whole. You are simply a cog in a machine, and your place is unfathomable to you. Greater wisdom had led you down your path and is continuing to lead you.

Acceptance of this fact and compassion with everything around you will illuminate your path further, and you will achieve your place within the world, as the universe desires. Along the way, you will achieve whatever your true purpose is.

It all begins with being present and accepting your situation. Allow external events to pass through you and remain grounded in the reality that the universe wants what's best for you and is showing you the way.

You just need to open your true sense of sight and look.

Conclusion

I s surrender a negative word? Within martial terms, perhaps yes, it is. In terms of the universe, though, it is far from it. The act of letting things pass through you, as discussed in the previous chapter, is an act of surrender.

This does not mean you remain passive in the face of aggression or accept defeat when present with adverse circumstances. It means you perform the right action, which is to say, you accept your emotions at the moment but don't identify with them. Emotions are illusory and will soon subside.

Continue to strive to improve your lot in life and realize that this improvement goes beyond the collection of material things which you think will provide you comfort. Read the signs that nature is providing you with and respond and react accordingly. Surrendering to your present situation is what enables you to stop making excuses and take responsibility for your situation.

This is how you set yourself on the path to right action and relieve yourself from negative pressure. A lot of people get down on themselves and paint themselves as victims. This is but the ego fooling you.

You are no victim. You are strong and have the backing of the most powerful force in the universe, which is to say, you are an extension of it and contain within you everything you need to achieve what you want.

You just need to open yourself up to it. Surrender and let it flow through you.